INSIDE MENNONITE LIFE AND THOUGHT

INSIDE MENNONITE LIFE AND THOUGHT

ANABAPTIST CORE BELIEFS

Karl R. Landis

Foreword by
Michele Hershberger

Publishing House
Telford, Pennsylvania

Cascadia Publishing House orders, information, reprint permissions:
contact@CascadiaPublishingHouse.com
1-215-723-9125
126 Klingerman Road, Telford PA 18969
www.CascadiaPublishingHouse.com

Inside Mennonite Life and Thought
Copyright © 2025 by Cascadia Publishing House LLC
Telford, PA 18969
All rights reserved
DreamSeeker Books is an imprint of Cascadia Publishing House LLC
ISBN 13: 978-1-68027-026-6

Book design by Cascadia Publishing House
Cover design by Gwen M. Stamm, based on
cover photo by Regina Jershova/Shutterstock

All Scripture quotations, unless otherwise indicated, are taken from the Holy Bible, New International Version®, NIV®. Copyright ©1973, 1978, 1984, 2011 by Biblica, Inc.™ Used by permission of Zondervan. All rights reserved worldwide. www.zondervan.com The "NIV" and "New International Version" are trademarks registered in the United States Patent and Trademark Office by Biblica, Inc.™. Quotations marked CEV are from the *Contemporary English Version*, Copyright © American Bible Society, 1995; NLT are taken from the Holy Bible, *New Living Translation*, copyright ©1996, 2004, 2015 by Tyndale House Foundation. Used by permission of Tyndale House Publishers, Carol Stream, Illinois 60188. All rights reserved; NRSV are from *The New Revised Standard Version of the Bible*, copyright 1989, by the Division of Christian Education of the National Council of the Churches of Christ in the USA.Text: Copyright © American Bible Society, 1995.

Library of Congress Cataloging-in-Publication Data
Names: Landis, Karl, 1961- author.
Title: Inside Mennnonite life and thought : Anabaptist core beliefs / Karl Landis.
Description: Telford, Pennsylvania : Cascadia Publishing House, [2025] | Includes bibliographical references. | Summary: "Landis explains what makes Mennonites and other Anabaptists unique. He argues that their practices are expressions of underlying beliefs based on the teachings and example of Jesus. Other Christians may not agree with given practices, but most will at least value the underlying core beliefs"-- Provided by publisher.
Identifiers: LCCN 2024061344 | ISBN 9781680270266 (trade paperback)
Subjects: LCSH: Mennonites--Doctrines. | Anabaptists--Doctrines.
Classification: LCC BX8121.3 .L36 2025 | DDC 230/.97--dc23/eng/20250216
LC record available at https://lccn.loc.gov/2024061344

*To Nita,
who has been gracious, kind, and patient through
many twists and turns*

Contents

Foreword by Michele Hershberger 7
Introduction 9

1 **CORE BELIEFS** 15
2 **JESUS IS LORD OVER ABSOLUTELY EVERYTHING** 28
   Core belief 1: Jesus Is Lord
3 **THE KINGDOM OF GOD IS WHERE PEOPLE UNITE UNDER THE LORDSHIP OF JESUS** 46
   Core belief 2: The Kingdom of God
4 **WE CHOOSE TO FOLLOW JESUS** 69
   Core belief 3: Choose
5 **WE FOLLOW JESUS IN EVERYDAY LIFE** 86
   Core belief 4: Follow
6 **WE FOLLOW JESUS TOGETHER** 101
   Core belief 5: Together
7 **WE SURRENDER OUR LIVES IN LOVE LIKE JESUS DID** 123
   Core belief 6: Surrender Our Lives in Love
8 **PRACTICES BASED ON THE CORE BELIEFS** 145
9 **ANABAPTIST CORE BELIEFS TODAY** 161

Appendix: References and Resources 174
The Author 181

Foreword

Recently I had the privilege of addressing a Mennonite conference on the early Anabaptist challenge to Christian nationalism. I proceeded with trepidation, for I'm not an historian. As I researched the early Anabaptists, I expected to find large and profound quotes from our early leaders on the dangers of a Christian nation. Menno Simons would say this and that, Michael Sattler would nuance the finer points, and all our early leaders would stress separation of church and state.

With a few exceptions, I didn't find much.

I did find many beautiful arguments on why we should only baptize believers and not swear oaths or take up the sword against our enemies. I did find implicit arguments against the separation of church and state. But for the most part, I found arguments for certain Christian practices based on Scripture and the primacy of Jesus for interpreting Scripture. At every turn, these arguments were based on Scripture.

My instincts say they didn't need to explicitly address the unholy connection between the state and the church. This critique didn't need saying; it was a natural outcome of their core understanding of how to read the Bible and the importance of following Jesus. Their worldview—what for the most part went unsaid—was that if the Scriptures disagree with each other, you follow Jesus. What went without being said was if your government told you to do one thing and Jesus told you to do another, you followed Jesus. What was seldom said but wholeheartedly understood was that if we gather as a local community, committed to finding the truth together, then we can discern God's will just as well as the church authorities. What went without being said was that we must do all of these things, even if it meant death.

And what needs to be said today is this: We must recapture this worldview, these underlying beliefs. We need to start saying aloud what in the past has gone without saying.

This is the gift Karl Landis has given us. He has written a book to remind us of the core beliefs and values that have shaped us into a distinct Christian movement. If basing one's beliefs on Scripture were all that was needed, then the task would be easy. People from every Christian tradition use Scripture to at least some extent. It's how we read Scripture; it's how we understand discipleship, how we understand community.

Landis reminds us that we center everything on Jesus. When the Scriptures disagree with each other, we follow Jesus. Like Jesus, we embrace a broader salvation, a salvation that doesn't just get us to heaven but works to bring physical and emotional salvation as well as spiritual healing. And this beautiful thing we call the Christian life is not just assenting to certain beliefs but to having a living relationship with the One who transforms us so we live out those six core beliefs. The practices flow naturally from our core beliefs and our reliance on the Spirit. And the transformation is so complete and the practices so genuine that people notice—they stop and stare.

In a word, says Landis, Jesus is *Lord* over everything.

Landis candidly admits we're far from perfect and authentically illuminates the complexities of our theology. But we do have a gift to give to the wider church and to the world. And we're different. Landis helps us understand these differences, whether we are unfamiliar with Anabaptist Mennonites or *are* one of those Anabaptist Mennonites who has lost their way.

My prayer is that you will hear what has been left unsaid, and on hearing that, by the power of the Spirit, together with your community, be transformed for service to the world.

—*Michele Hershberger, Bible and Ministry Professor and Co-Campus Pastor, Hesston (Kan.) College*

Introduction

As I was wrapping up the last session of a new members' class for our Mennonite church some years ago, a young woman who grew up in a Southern Baptist church asked, "When are we going to get to the weird stuff?" She had been part of our life together for several years, she loved the people of our congregation, and she was ready to join us as a member, but she still had a sense that there was something weird or odd about Mennonites in general that we had failed to cover in the class. Several years later, I heard someone else say, "I can't believe I'm attending a *Mennonite* church!"

Over the years, I have come to realize that Mennonites are often seen as unusual because, in the minds of outsiders, Mennonites have often been mainly associated with non-participation in the military and with very drab or plain clothing (and sometimes confused with the Amish). What many people don't realize is that these practices are not simply ways for contrarians to be countercultural (or weird!). They are actually outward expressions of beliefs that are at the core of the Mennonite understanding of the life and teachings of Jesus and his apostles in the New Testament.

As a pastor and teacher, I have wrestled with how to provide a brief, clear, and memorable summary of what those core beliefs are and how they are connected to the practices that have made Mennonites sometimes look or seem different from other Christians. I want to help people outside the Mennonite world understand us from the inside, to summarize or explain this approach to following Jesus in clear and simple terms, so they can appreciate its strengths and its contributions to the body of Christ. I have wished that I had a short book I could use in a new members' class to help explain these things to people who have little or no familiarity with Mennonite life and thought.

Of course, it's also important to present a clear and compelling summary of the core beliefs of Mennonite life and thought to Mennonites themselves, because, like people everywhere, we tend to settle into our habits, and the reasons for those habits fade if we fail to review them and celebrate them. It's important to regularly remind ourselves of our core beliefs, so that we and our children can continue to understand and grow in our appreciation for what we believe and why we practice our faith in the way we do.

So here we go! This book is my summary of six core beliefs that provide the grounding for Mennonite life and thought as we seek to follow Jesus in ways that are consistent with and faithful to the emphases of the New Testament. Once you understand the six core beliefs, I am confident you will see how the practices flow from the beliefs.

It's worth noting at the outset that these core beliefs and the practices derived from them are not as unusual among Christians as they once were, especially in the Western world. I'll have more to say about that in chapter 9 after we review each of the core beliefs.

It's also worth noting that this book is written for a general audience rather than for scholars. This means that my focus is on presenting a cohesive overview rather than a detailed picture of all the nuances and differences between various Anabaptist groups, of which I assure you there are many! (Mennonites are one type of "Anabaptist.") It also means that I'll be painting with a fairly broad brush. I'm not claiming to speak with authority for every person or group who see themselves as Anabaptist, even though I have walked with, talked with, and learned from thousands of my fellow Anabaptists from all over the world. There will always be exceptions to general summary statements.

It may be helpful for you to know that I write from a particular vantage point. Most of my lived experience of the Anabaptist world has been shaped by the understandings and lives of Mennonites in what used to be known as "the Mennonite Church." Most of the Mennonites I know best are from south-central or southeastern Pennsylvania—Franklin County (where I was born) and Lancaster County (where I have lived)—and their Mennonite conferences. And even though I have been deeply impacted by Mennonites from a wide range of cultural backgrounds and from many different countries, my deeper experience and familiarity is with Mennonites who are ethnically Swiss German. This has affected the concepts I use, the language I share them in, and the reality that some Mennonites might approach some things differently.

The framework of core beliefs presented here is drawn from my own analysis of how the pieces fit together in Anabaptist thought and life, both historically and in the present. It's how I connect the dots in a way that I believe is accurate and faithful to the inner workings of this particular approach to Christian faith and discipleship. My hope is to clarify misunderstandings about it that I have encountered both outside and inside the Anabaptist world. I hope you find it encouraging, challenging, and inspiring.

Note on Mennonites and Anabaptists

One of the distinctions I learned to make clearly in our new members' classes was that Mennonites are ANA-baptists, not ANTI-baptists. *Ana* is a prefix from Latin that means to repeat or do again. So Anabaptists were considered RE-baptizers by their enemies, but they were not and never have been "opponents of baptizers." The term *Anabaptist* was initially a slur directed at the Swiss Germans who, in 1525, began baptizing adults when they professed a personal faith in Jesus.

Although baptizing adult converts doesn't seem at all strange to most people today, these adults had all been baptized as infants and were already considered Christians by the laws and customs of the time. But when the Anabaptists could find no instruction in the New Testament to baptize infants, they began to teach that infant baptism was not a valid baptism. They pointed out that all of the baptisms and teachings about baptism recorded in the New Testament describe baptism as the next step for new believers, and they began to teach that the only valid Christian baptism is the baptism of believers. As a result, they baptized adult believers and did not have their babies baptized. This directly challenged the teaching and practice of both the Catholic and reforming churches and defied the authority of the city councils that were defending infant baptism.

Adult baptism disrupted the close partnership and intertwining of church and government that was upheld and defended by leaders in both institutions. The early Anabaptists were denounced and then persecuted by church and government leaders for their refusal to comply with the restrictions on baptism, evangelism, and communion ordered by the ruling councils. They were condemned as insurrectionists because their ideas were upsetting the established order of their towns.

Three groups of the descendants of those early Anabaptists immigrated to the Americas in the 1700s and 1800s—the Mennonites, the Amish, and the Hutterites. These groups mostly agree on the six core beliefs presented here, but they live them out differently. When people—here in Lancaster County, Pennsylvania where I now live—ask me how Mennonites differ from the Amish, I usually say we are theological cousins who share core beliefs, but who live them out differently. Other Anabaptist groups today include the Brethren in Christ, the Church of the Brethren, Mennonite Brethren, among others.

When Mennonites refer to our theological perspective as "Anabaptist," we are linking our approach to theology to a framework first articulated in the 1520s by the Swiss Germans described earlier. So, Mennonites are a subset of Anabaptists, but not all Anabaptists are Mennonites.

Chapter 1

Core Beliefs

The person, example, teachings, death, resurrection, and ascension of Jesus to supreme lordship provide the primary basis for Anabaptist beliefs and teaching.

Martin Luther had no intention of breaking away from the Roman Catholic Church when he posted his 95 Theses in 1517. The 95 Theses document was a list of statements and questions challenging the church's support for teachings and practices not taught in Scripture. His goal was to reform the church from within. Luther was calling the church to live up to its ideals.

In much the same way, the early Anabaptists were not hoping to break away from the already reforming church being guided by their primary mentor, Ulrich Zwingli. They were inspired and excited by the changes Zwingli had made to align the teaching and practice of the church with the New Testament. But they soon discovered that he was willing to limit the changes to ones that would be acceptable to local government officials.

There were two main stumbling blocks for the early Anabaptists in Zurich in 1525. The first was that Zwingli was willing to let the city council decide which changes to the teachings and practices of the church would be permitted and which would not. The second, a specific example of the first, was that the city council was unwilling to reject infant baptism in favor of believers baptism. The early Anabaptists considered both of these matters to be direct contradictions to the teaching and practice of Jesus and the apostles.

Creedal Beliefs

None of the reformers in the early 1500s rejected the foundational Christian doctrines summarized in the early creeds of the church. The problem for them was that, as they read the Bible for themselves, they realized that over the centuries, the Roman Catholic Church had embraced teachings and practices that seemed to change the message of the New Testament.

For example, many of Martin Luther's 95 Theses protested the sale of indulgences. In the early 1500s, the church was raising money for, among other things, the construction of Saint Peter's Basilica in Rome. One important fundraiser was the sale of certificates, called indulgences, that promised both forgiveness for the purchaser's sins and exemption from purgatory after death.

The church taught that Christians spend the time between their physical death and their entry into heaven in a place called "purgatory" where their souls would be fully purged of earthly attachments in preparation for being admitted to heaven. The more purging you needed, the more time you would spend in purgatory. By purchasing an indulgence, you could literally buy forgiveness for your sins from the church and reduce the amount of time you would spend in purgatory. You could also buy indulgences for the sins of your loved ones, including loved ones who had died and who might be suffering in purgatory.

Luther spoke for many when he objected to this teaching and practice as unbiblical and contrary to both the spirit and the substance of the gospel message. He also objected to the general notion of earning your salvation by good works of any sort, arguing that the New Testament clearly teaches that our sins are forgiven and we are saved only by the grace of God. As other priests and preachers began to read and interpret the Scriptures for themselves, they also objected to other teachings and practices not clearly taught in the New Testament.

Ulrich Zwingli was one such pastor and preacher in Zurich, Switzerland. He was inspired by Luther but also disagreed with him at times. Zwingli persuaded the local authorities to allow him to preach directly from the Scriptures and to make changes to Sunday worship services and the serving of communion. The earliest Anabaptists were followers of Zwingli who eventually broke from him when they realized he was willing to limit the reforms to changes that gained the approval of Zurich's city council. They rejected that restriction as unbiblical, especially when it limited their exploration of fully aligning their teaching and practice with the New Testament.

Zwingli, Zurich's city council, and other reformers quickly denounced these early Anabaptists as heretics. They accused the Anabaptists of rejecting sound Christian teaching, even though, as we will see, they led a rapidly growing movement of people whose lives were dramatically changed by the power of the Holy Spirit at work within, among, and through them. The notion that Anabaptists were wild-eyed heretics persisted in studies of church history well into the 1900s. Even today, one Lutheran denomination's website refers to Anabaptists as "false teachers," describes their teachings as "heresy," and says, "Nowadays, the Anabaptistic heresy is taught amongst the Mennonites, the Amish, and the Swiss Brethren." So it may be helpful to review how Anabaptists understand basic Christian beliefs!

Let's start with this one: Anabaptists are trinitarians. That is, we believe, along with our orthodox brothers and sisters in Christ, that God has revealed himself, the one true and living God, to be Father, Son, and Holy Spirit. No one had any notion of God-as-Trinity before Jesus. But as the earliest church leaders grappled with the life and teachings and work of Jesus, especially in light of his resurrection and ascension, they eventually came to the conclusion that God-as-Trinity was the only faithful and accurate way to fit the pieces together. Anabaptists affirm the creedal beliefs of Christians about the trinitarian God. These have been rearticulated in the first three articles of the *Confession of Faith in a Mennonite Perspective* (1995).

At the same time, the early Anabaptists pointed out that the Apostles' Creed and the Nicene Creed both jump directly from Jesus' birth to his death. Both creeds ignore his life and his teachings and thereby omit any mention of his mission of calling together a people who would live transformed lives as the people of God. Even though this was a central focus of Jesus' teaching, *the kingdom of God made visible in the transformed life of the people of God* has too often been overlooked by Christians over the centuries.

Anabaptists also hold a high view of Scripture as the trustworthy word of God. The earliest Anabaptists memorized large portions of Scripture, using it as the basis for their quest to reexamine every belief and teaching and practice of the church to see which ones were and which ones were not solidly based on Scripture.

If you read through their responses to the charges and objections of their opponents, you will find that their most frequent defense is an appeal to the Scriptures as the final authority over the teachings and practices of the church. What they say over and over again, in my paraphrase, is "Show me what you are saying in the Scriptures, and I will agree with you." As Menno Simons, an early Anabaptist leader, put it, "We neither have, nor know any other positions, faith, or doctrine than that which may be plainly read, heard, and understood... from the word of God" (Simons 1539, 108).

In a dispute with a Protestant reformer named Oecolampad over the validity of infant baptism, Anabaptist Balthasar Hubmaier challenged his opponent to join him in "presenting ourselves... before the judgment chair of holy Scripture." He went on to say, "Either you must point out with a clear Scripture where God has instituted infant baptism or it must be rooted out.... I will trust Cyprian [a bishop in the early 200s], councils, and other teachings just as far as they use the holy Scripture and not more." He then makes the larger point: "To overthrow a practice which is not instituted in Scripture is not an abuse, but a command of Christ" (Freeman 1999, 33-36).

All of the reformers in the early 1500s agreed that the authority of Scripture supersedes the authority of the church (church officials). That was their main and very contentious point of departure from Roman Catholic teaching. According to Catholic teaching, the head(s) of the Catholic Church inherits the authority of Jesus on the earth. That means the pope and the bishops in union with him carry the authority of Jesus in making decisions about what constitutes faithful teaching and practice in the kingdom of God while we anticipate Jesus' return. In that sense, Roman Catholics consider the authority of the overall leadership of the church to be equal to the authority of the Scriptures. Both are considered equally authoritative in determining the beliefs and practices of the faithful.

While Protestants and Anabaptists then and now respect the authority of church leaders, they disagree that church leaders ever bear the full authority of Jesus in interpreting or extending Christian teaching beyond what we find in the Scriptures. In other words, Protestants and Anabaptists consider Christian leaders to be fully under the authority of Scripture and hold that Christian teaching and practice should always be grounded in or disciplined by Scripture (*COF* 1995, Article 4).

One problem the reformers soon faced among themselves was that they did not agree with each other on which scriptural teachings were centrally important. For Luther the grace of God provided the central focus from which he reconsidered all Christian theology. For Calvin several decades later, the sovereignty of God provided the central focus and organizing principle for his understanding and teaching. For the Anabaptists, the starting point and organizing principle was Jesus—his lordship, his example, and his teachings.

Another problem the other reformers had with the Anabaptists was disagreement over the relationship between the Old and New Testaments. Protestants and Catholics mostly considered the two covenants (Old and New) to be equal in authority. Anabaptists, on the other hand, saw the New Testament as having authority over the Old Testament in interpretation, largely because Jesus himself referred to the covenant of Moses as *old* and to his covenant as *new* (Matt. 13:52, Luke 22:20).

Hubmaier illustrates this difference clearly when he says, in his debate with Oecolampad, "Water baptism is a ceremony of the New Testament. Therefore I demand from you a clear word out of the New Testament with which you bring to us this infant baptism. But you prove infant baptism from Exodus" (Freeman 1999, 39).

The reformers all agreed that the Scriptures were authoritative as God's Word to us. But because they approached their study of the Scriptures with different central focuses and organizing principles in mind, they came to hold overlapping but sometimes rather different understandings of sin, salvation, the second coming, baptism, communion, and the nature of the church (see *COF* 1995).

Some of the differences were only subtle, but others were significant enough that some of the reformers accused others of heresy. Luther, Melanchthon, Zwingli, Bullinger, and later Calvin, harshly and vehemently denounced the Anabaptists as heretics of the worst kind. Luther and the others had little tolerance for differing approaches to Christian faith and life. They feared that Anabaptist convictions would completely upend the order of civil society.

Anabaptist Core Beliefs

The person, example, teachings, death, resurrection, and ascension of Jesus to supreme lordship provide the primary focus of Anabaptist beliefs and teaching.

Menno Simons, the early Anabaptist leader from whom the name *Mennonite* is derived, repeatedly emphasized in his preaching and writing that true Christian faith is faith that proclaims no more and no less than what Jesus and his apostles lived and taught.

> Ministers who can rightly be called Christian . . . are so [fully devoted to] the word and truth of the Lord that they dare not teach or preach a word other than Christ Jesus himself has taught, practiced, and commanded, namely, the pure, unadulterated, biblical word in the true sense and meaning of Christ and of his holy apostles. . . . (Simons 1544, 440-441)

Simons's appeal went much further than just basing beliefs and practices on biblical proof texts. His appeal was for all Christians to believe and then to live out the Christian way "in the true sense and meaning" of the Scriptures intended by Jesus and his apostles. His test for biblical interpretation was something like, "Is our interpretation of Scripture faithful to the nature and character of Jesus?" or "Is our interpretation in harmony with what Jesus intended?"

Elsewhere he writes

> I would rather die than to believe and teach . . . a single word concerning the Father, the Son, and the Holy Ghost, [that is] at variance with the express testimony of God's Word, as it is so clearly given through the mouth of prophets, evangelists and apostles. (Simons 1550, 497)

And [if our opponents]

> can support their teachings with the Word and command of God, we will admit that they are right. If not, then [their teachings are] a doctrine of men and accursed according to the Scriptures. (Simons 1554, 695)

Simons's favorite verse, which appeared on the flyleaf of each of his books, made this point very clearly: "For no one can lay any foundation other than the one already laid, which is Jesus Christ" (1 Cor. 3:11). He was voicing the concerns widely shared by Anabaptists that a.) the Christian teachers of their time had added many things to the simple gospel preached by Jesus, and b.) the behavior of many people claiming to be Christians looked nothing at all like the life Jesus lived and called his followers to live.

The primary focus of the preaching of the early Anabaptists was calling people to turn away from the extra-biblical practices that had been added to the gospel, to turn away from sin, and to surrender their lives fully to Jesus. They believed, based on the teachings of the New Testament, that when people were truly converted, their lives would be transformed and would produce the results Jesus called for in his teachings.

The goal of the early Anabaptists was to reexamine and reorient everything in Christian life and thought to be in harmony with the example and teachings of Jesus and his apostles. They called people to think and teach and live, as much as humanly possible and by the power of the Holy Spirit, exactly and only what Jesus and his apostles thought and taught and lived, and to reject all the extras that had been added to that teaching over the centuries.

Here is a three sentence summary of their underlying system of core beliefs. Think of it as a brief outline of their understanding of the heart of New Testament Christian faith. Their focus was not on creating their own denomination nor on being different from other Christians. Their focus was on articulating Christian life and thought as intended and modeled by Jesus and his apostles.

- *Jesus is Lord over absolutely everything.*
- *The kingdom of God is where people unite under the lordship of Jesus.*
- *We choose to follow Jesus together, surrendering our lives in love like he did.*

The first statement is the most important. It provides the focal point for everything that follows in our thinking, in our theology, in our churches, and in every part of our lives. If Jesus really is Lord over absolutely everything, then there's nothing in our lives, nothing in the lives of other people, nothing in the world, and nothing in all creation over which Jesus is not Lord. That means that we will properly understand or properly engage anything at all only when we understand it or engage it through or under the lordship of Jesus.

The second statement acknowledges that, even though Jesus is Lord over absolutely everything, not everyone is cooperating with or surrendering to his lordship. Not everyone has said yes to his call to "repent, believe, and follow me." A primary focus of Jesus' ministry was calling people to become part of the kingdom of God that he had come to inaugurate. The first two statements listed here provide the underpinnings for everything else that follows.

The third statement summarizes what it means to say yes to Jesus' call, to become his followers as described in the New Testament by Jesus and his apostles. As we choose to follow Jesus and join together as his people, we follow his example in surrendering our lives in love to each other and to the world around us like he did.

This summary is my formulation and my wording. It's based on my study and analysis of Anabaptist history and theology and on my attempts to provide a clear, concise, and compelling summary of our beliefs and practices as a preacher and teacher. Most of what you will read about our faith tradition jumps to the third of the statements, paying less careful attention to its basis in the first two statements. So conversion, discipleship, humility, and service show up frequently in these presentations, but my contention is that these can only be properly understood as the outworking of the first two statements.

Often the lordship of Jesus and the kingdom of God are jumbled in with other topics. My claim is that these are the primary underlying convictions that provide the grounding for all of the other beliefs and all the practices derived from them. My further claim is that even when Anabaptist writers don't specifically mention the lordship of Jesus and the kingdom of God, those two beliefs provide the animating force of their preaching and writing.

In the following restatement of the three sentences, I have bolded the words that summarize the six core beliefs captured by these sentences.

- ***Jesus is Lord*** *over absolutely everything.*
- *The **kingdom of God** is where people unite under the lordship of Jesus.*
- *We **choose to follow Jesus together, surrendering our lives in love** like he did.*

It might be more helpful to see the core beliefs expressed as six separate statements. Here is a simple expansion of the three sentences into six.

1. **Jesus is Lord** over absolutely everything.
2. The **kingdom of God** is where people unite under the lordship of Jesus.
3. We **choose** to follow Jesus.
4. We **follow Jesus** in everyday life.
5. We follow Jesus **together**.
6. We **surrender our lives in love** like Jesus did.

The next six chapters of this book (chapters 2-7) focus on each of these core beliefs one at a time. I explain them more fully and provide the scriptural grounding for each one. I also show how each one flows into the next.

A Crucial Point to Understand

You may be wondering why plain (or drab) clothing, declining to join the military, and washing each other's feet (what you may think of as the weird stuff!) are not mentioned in any of the six statements. That's because plain dress, refusing military service, and foot washing are just some of the specific ways Anabaptist followers of Jesus have chosen to put their core beliefs *into practice*. They are *practices* based on underlying *beliefs*. They are not *core beliefs* themselves.

Some Anabaptist practices are based on direct commands from Jesus. For example, we take Jesus literally when he says, "Now that I, your Lord and Teacher, have washed your feet, you also should wash one another's feet. I have set you an example that you should do as I have done for you" (John 13:14-15). As a result, many Mennonites and other Anabaptist groups offer at least occasional foot washing opportunities, usually connected to their worship services.

Foot washing is sometimes linked to communion services and sometimes to Maundy Thursday services in commemoration of the last supper where Jesus washed the feet of his disciples and gave the instruction recorded by John. Washing each other's feet is a very specific way of expressing our willingness to obey our Lord's commands (Jesus is Lord / we follow him), and our willingness to surrender our lives in love like he did.

Other Anabaptist practices are attempts to live out the core beliefs in a particular time and place. For example, we think Jesus meant it when he said, "Love your enemies" (Luke 6:27, 35). He went on to say in that same passage that he meant you should "do good to those who hate you, bless those who curse you, [and] pray for those who mistreat you."

Concluding that it is impossible for a soldier to obey this command from Jesus, many Anabaptists have refused to participate in the military. In a broader application, we have rejected destructive violence in resolving disputes with other people since that also directly contradicts Jesus' instructions to his followers. These practices are two more ways we express our willingness to obey our Lord's commands (Jesus is Lord / we follow him), and our willingness to surrender our lives in love like he did.

I will discuss the relationship between core beliefs and practices in more detail in Chapter 8, but here is an overview of what may be the most important point for understanding Mennonite life and thought from the inside:

If you are a follower of Jesus, you probably agree in a general sense with the six core beliefs I have listed above. As long as these beliefs are all just abstract ideas, they are not very controversial among Christians. Abstractions don't usually get people into trouble. The trouble starts when we begin to talk about how to put those ideas into practice in our everyday lives.

The deeper challenge is that these particular beliefs only have their full meaning in the real world if you live them out in some way. That is, they are meant to be visibly expressed in your daily life. In other words, you have to "do the beliefs" if you want them to be fully real. These six core beliefs each have direct implications for daily life, so you have to express them in specific practices for them to become real in your life.

The central misunderstanding about Mennonites and a central problem within Mennonite faith communities has been that too many of our practices have taken on a life of their own. We have treated them as core beliefs rather than as applications *of core beliefs.*

We have too often failed to clearly distinguish between our beliefs and the practices that express our beliefs in everyday life. When the practices become ends in themselves, we eventually lose touch with why we developed them in the first place.

For example, foot washing and not participating in the military are not ends in themselves. They don't stand alone as Anabaptist convictions. Both of them are grounded in underlying core beliefs. Both of them are ways of expressing our willingness to obey our Lord's commands (core belief 1: Jesus is Lord / core belief 4: We follow / obey him), and our willingness to surrender our lives in love like he did (core belief 6).

Plain dress is another example. Wearing plain (or drab) clothing grew out of a sincere desire to make a shared announcement about being fully surrendered to Jesus. The goal was to turn away together from being so concerned about one's outward appearance and from the cost of keeping up with fashion trends. The early proponents of plain dress saw it as part of being different from the world around them and part of being wholehearted in their united surrender to the call of Jesus on their lives. Plain dress is a practice that makes concrete a commitment to follow Jesus together in rejecting worldly standards (core beliefs 4 and 5) and a willingness to surrender our lives in love like he did (core belief 6).

So far so good. The problem was that over time, within some Anabaptist faith communities, plain dress came to be seen as a clear marker for who was and who was not willing to be fully committed to Jesus. In a tightly knit community, people who wanted to express their full surrender in other ways were a problem, because plain dress had become one of the shared expectations for how to express your surrender to Jesus together with other believers. A willingness to surrender to the church (in how you dress) became an important way to put your surrender to Jesus into practice. Plain dress has sometimes been a shared practice among some Anabaptist groups and remains so for a variety of them as a way to express one or more of our core beliefs. But plain dress is not directly taught in the New Testament and is not a core belief of Anabaptists.

Summary

Mennonites in particular, and Anabaptists in general, embrace the basic trinitarian Christian beliefs presented in the Apostles' Creed and the Nicene Creed. Those beliefs are echoed and restated in the first five articles of our *Confession of Faith* (1995).

We further believe that in their teaching and writings, Jesus and his apostles particularly emphasized that
- Jesus is Lord over absolutely everything.
- The kingdom of God is where people unite under the lordship of Jesus.
- We choose to follow Jesus together, surrendering our lives in love like he did.

We embrace these teachings as essential starting points for how to live the life Jesus had in mind when he called people (now including you and me) to become his disciples.

We also seek to live out these core beliefs in specific, practical ways in our daily lives. That is, we don't only follow Jesus in a spiritual, inner, or private way. We believe that, according to the New Testament, following Jesus will reshape every aspect of our lives, resulting in practices that give our beliefs their full meaning in the real world. Another way to say that: If we are truly following Jesus in the way he intended, our lives will not make much sense to someone who knows nothing about his life and teachings.

NOTES: Unless otherwise indicated, all mentions of "our Confession of Faith," "the Confession of Faith," or COF refer to the Confession of Faith in a Mennonite Perspective *(1995).*

You can read a Mennonite restatement of creedal Christian beliefs about God (as Father, Son, Holy Spirit) and the Scriptures in the Confession of Faith in a Mennonite Perspective, *articles 1-5. Also see article 13: Foot washing, and article 22: Peace, justice, and nonresistance.*

Chapter 2

Jesus Is Lord Over Absolutely Everything

Core belief 1: Jesus Is Lord

On May 6, 2023, Charles the Third was crowned king of England. That means he is now properly known as His Majesty, Charles the Third, by the Grace of God, King of the United Kingdom of Great Britain and Northern Ireland and of His other Realms and Territories, Head of the Commonwealth, Defender of the Faith. That's a very impressive title.

King Charles's coronation ceremony was conducted as a Christian worship service led by the archbishop of Canterbury, primary leader of the Church of England. A Church of England statement explains that "The [coronation] liturgy is focused on the theme of loving service to others, which is central to Christian teaching, and to the character of contemporary monarchy."

What was really interesting to me is that if you listen to all the statements made during this Christian worship service, you will notice that they are designed to do several things:
- Acknowledge the even more important lordship or kingship of Jesus Christ (In other words, Charles is not the most important king.)
- Proclaim that God has called Charles to be King of the United Kingdom (In other words, God is on his side. Charles has been called and is being commissioned by God for this role.)

- Define Charles's responsibility to carry out God's purposes for him and for the United Kingdom (In other words, he is expected to live up to someone else's [God's] expectations for what he does or doesn't do as King. He isn't free to do whatever he wants to.)

You will also notice that the King of England doesn't crown himself. He receives the crown from someone else. So yes, Charles is now the king and that's important, but he answers to a higher king. I'm not sure how many people in the cathedral that day (including Charles himself) or how many people watching on TV really believe that, but at least that's what the words said.

Here are two examples of the statements that acknowledge the limits of Charles's lordship:

The section of the liturgy titled "The Anointing" is considered the most sacred part of the service. At this point, the king kneels (a physical expression of submission or surrender) to be anointed with oil as a sign of being commissioned for service to God. The wording of the blessing asks God to help this earthly king rule a temporal kingdom well and to later welcome the king into God's eternal kingdom.

The archbishop pronounces the following blessing after he has anointed the king with oil on his hands, his chest, and his head:

> Our Lord Jesus Christ, the Son of God, who by his Father was anointed with the oil of gladness above his fellows, by his holy anointing pour down upon your head and heart the blessing of the Holy Spirit, and prosper the works of your hands, that by the assistance of his heavenly grace you may govern and preserve the people committed to your charge in wealth, peace, and godliness; and after a long and glorious course of ruling a temporal kingdom wisely, justly, and religiously, you may at last be made partaker of an eternal kingdom, through the same Jesus Christ our Lord. Amen.

The archbishop (in his words) and Charles (in his actions of kneeling and receiving) acknowledge the higher authority and lordship of "Jesus Christ our Lord" and announce that Charles is being commissioned on behalf of Jesus and in much the same way that Jesus himself was commissioned for service. This ceremony of commissioning reminds everyone, including Charles, that his kingship was not his idea and that he is expected to live up to standards provided by someone outside himself (God's standards). The archbishop says that we want God to bless and help Charles to carry the responsibilities and carry out the duties of his assigned role in this temporal kingdom.

When the liturgy finally gets to "The Crowning," the archbishop pronounces another prayer of blessing. It's written and recited in King James English, so here is my paraphrase of what it says:

> King of kings and lord of lords, we ask you to bless this crown and your servant, Charles, with your favor, with your grace, and with all princely virtues. . . . [We ask this] through our Lord Jesus Christ, your Son, who lives and reigns with you in the unity of the Holy Spirit, one God, for ever and ever.

Here we, and Charles, receive one final reminder that Charles isn't the highest king, that he will be expected to live up to someone else's (God's) standards, that he will need God's help to rule well as an earthly king.

It's pretty remarkable that the crowning of the king of England is framed so clearly as a commissioning by and on behalf of a higher king. I expected the language of the liturgy to be more triumphant and assertive about the power and authority being conferred on the king, but instead it very strongly asserts his subservience to a higher king, the King of Kings and Lord of Lords, to whom this earthly king is expected to answer.

If you wonder why the liturgy is framed this way, it's because it's faithful to what the New Testament says about Jesus. The phrasings, at least the ones about Jesus, come directly from the book of Revelation (King of Kings and Lord of Lords—17:14, 19:16). Revelation 11:15 says, "The kingdoms of this world are become the kingdoms of our Lord, and of his Christ; and he shall reign for ever and ever" (KJV).

The Lordship of Jesus

Christian teaching and imagery about the lordship of Jesus are based on Jesus' own statements and on the reflections of his apostles after his ascension from the earth. The apostles frequently link Jesus' resurrection and his ascension to the right hand of God as the two main insights their hearers need to understand about the end of his ministry on earth. Their frequent reference to him in their writings as "our Lord Jesus Christ" reminds everyone of his continuing role and authority.

Jesus' most frequent description of himself was as "the Son of man." Every time he referred to himself using that phrase, he was repeating an announcement that he was fulfilling part of the ancient prophetic vision recorded in the book of Daniel chapter 7. In verses 13 and 14, Daniel says he saw someone who looked like a human being (he looked like "a son of man") who was led into the presence of the Almighty God. Daniel watched in astonishment as that person was given the authority of God, the power of God, and even the right to share in receiving the worship of God. He says this "son of man" was given a permanent dominion over all things.

> In my vision at night I looked, and there before me was one like a son of man, coming with the clouds of heaven. He approached the Ancient of Days and was led into his presence. He was given authority, glory and sovereign power; all nations and peoples of every language worshiped him. His dominion is an everlasting dominion that will not pass away, and his kingdom is one that will never be destroyed. I, Daniel, was troubled in spirit, and the visions that passed through my mind disturbed me. (Dan. 7:13-14)

The writers of the New Testament along with Jesus himself point to his supreme lordship whenever they describe him as "seated at the right hand of God." That phrase is a poetic way of saying that Jesus has the highest possible honor and the highest possible authority. It means Jesus shares in God's strength, authority, and blessing. It means that all other things and all other beings are under Him. For example, 1 Peter 3:22 says that Jesus

Christ "has gone into heaven and is at God's right hand—with angels, authorities and powers in submission to him."
- At his trial before his death, Jesus links these two terms when he says, "From now on, **the Son of man** will be **seated at the right hand of the mighty God**" (Luke 22:69).
- Sometime in the days between his resurrection and his ascension, Jesus said to his disciples, in the version of the great commission recorded by Matthew, "**All authority in heaven and on earth has been given to me.** Therefore go and make disciples of all nations, baptizing them in the name of the Father and of the Son and of the Holy Spirit, and teaching them to obey everything I have commanded you. And surely I am with you always, to the very end of the age" (Matt. 28:18-20).
- On the day of Pentecost, Peter tells the crowd of curious onlookers that what they are witnessing is the result of the trinitarian God's purposes in the resurrection and ascension of Jesus: "God has raised this Jesus to life, and we are all witnesses of it. **Exalted to the right hand of God,** he has received from the Father the promised Holy Spirit and has poured out what you now see and hear" (Acts 2:32-33).
- Paul opens his letter to the church in Ephesus with a prayer that the believers there would personally experience the "incomparably great power" of God. He says, "That power is the same as the mighty strength he exerted when he raised Christ from the dead and **seated him at his right hand** in the heavenly realms, **far above all rule and authority, power and dominion, and every name that is invoked**, not only in the present age but also in the one to come. And **God placed all things under his feet and appointed him to be head over everything** for the church, which is his body, the fullness of him who fills everything in every way" (Eph. 1:19-23).

This is what Jesus has been doing since his ascension. This is what he *is* doing right now. Jesus is ruling over (he is far above) every ruler, every authority, every power, every leader—over everything. Jesus is Lord over absolutely everything. That doesn't mean that everything that happens is directed by him. It just means that the deepest truth about power and authority in our world is that the power and authority of Jesus is far greater than any other power or authority we know. That's true now (in the present age), and it will be true in perpetuity (in the age to come).

Acts 1 tells us that forty days after Jesus was raised from the dead, he ascended into heaven. He was bodily lifted from the earth and rose through the air until his closest followers who were with him that day could not see him anymore. Ever since, followers of Jesus all around the world remember that event when we celebrate Ascension Day. Ascension Day may be the most important neglected Christian holiday. It's actually a crucial day for us to remember, a day to retell the story and to worship, since it's a day to focus on honoring and celebrating the lordship of Jesus Christ. For the apostles, if part one of Jesus' exaltation was his resurrection, part two was his ascension to supreme lordship.

Anabaptists agree with the Church of England that the authority and power of every earthly ruler is limited in scope and time, subordinate, and inferior by far to the all-encompassing authority and power of our Lord Jesus Christ. The continuing lordship of Jesus Christ over all things is the most important core belief we draw from the New Testament. Everything else we believe and teach flows from the reality that Jesus really is Lord over absolutely everything.

To be clear, I'm not saying that the lordship of Jesus was cited in the early statements of Anabaptist beliefs as the explicit grounding of the Anabaptist framework. I'm suggesting that it was a deeper conviction that lay behind or beneath all of what they did articulate.

For example, Peter Riedeman said, we "confess [Christ] to be Lord; as, indeed, he truly is, for all power is given him by the Father, not only in heaven but also on earth and in the abyss" (Riedeman 1542, 31). Dirk Phillips wrote,

> We believe and confess that Jesus is our Lord and Savior, . . . divine from the beginning of the world and from eternity, and inexpressibly born of the Father, and one

Being with the Father, in such manner that they are one God and Lord, having equal power, might, love, glory, work, and will together eternally. (Philips 1557, 36)

Here's how Menno Simons put it in his *Confession of the Triune God:*

[The Scriptures testify that Christ Jesus] "formed heaven and earth, that he has all power in heaven and on earth, that he is the first and the last; that he tries the hearts and [reigns]; that it is he whom we should serve and worship; that he is the truth, the one who forgives sins and bestows eternal life, in whom we must believe." (Simons 1550, 494)

The lordship of Jesus provided and still provides the main underpinning for all of the implications I review below, each of which has been deeply formative in the life and thought of Anabaptists. Here's how the *Confession of Faith* summarizes it:

We worship Jesus Christ as the one whom God has exalted and made Lord over all. He is our Lord and the not-yet-recognized Lord of the world. . . . He is the one who shall be acknowledged Lord of all, and the Lamb who will reign forever and ever. (*COF* 1995, 14)

Okay, but why is that important?

Well, think about who or what is the most powerful person or ruler you can imagine. We usually think of nations, empires, and military power as the most powerful authorities.

During Jesus' time on earth, the most powerful ruler in the world was Caesar Augustus, the emperor of the Roman Empire. As head of the Roman Empire, the decisions Caesar Augustus made impacted everyone throughout most of what it now Europe, northern Africa, and the Middle East. Paul is saying that, even if it doesn't look like it, the truth is that Jesus' power and authority is far greater than Caesar Augustus's power and authority.

In the early 1200s, a conqueror emerged who was known as the "Universal Ruler." The words carrying that meaning in his own language were "Genghis Khan." Because of the power he amassed, he was considered the representative on earth of the supreme god of the Mongols whose destiny was to rule the world. His powerful and merciless army extended his rule from Mongolia all across central Asia, reaching the whole way to Europe. Eventually, the Mongols dominated the major trade centers of China, all of Asia, and Eastern Europe including Russia. The Mongol Empire was the largest and most powerful the world had ever seen. Paul is saying that, even if it doesn't look like it, the truth is that Jesus' power and authority is far greater than Genghis Khan's power and authority.

In the 1800s, another empire emerged that had even more power and controlled even more territory than the Mongol empire. At its peak, the British Empire controlled an estimated twenty-five percent of the world's land and twenty percent of the world's population. It was the financial center of the world. The king (or queen) of England was the most powerful person in the world. Paul is saying that, even if it doesn't look like it, the truth is that Jesus' power and authority is far greater than king or queen of England's power and authority is or ever has been.

Today, the president of the United States is considered the most powerful person in the world, because the United States dominates the world's economic and political order. The U.S. has the world's largest economy, the most powerful military, many of the best universities, and through the U.S. dollar the currency of international finance. Even though the United States may not control other nations directly in the way previous empires did, it maintains more than 750 military installations in more than eighty countries around the world, which is far more than any previous nation or empire. But Paul says that Jesus' power and authority is far greater than the U.S. president's power and authority is or ever has been.

Jesus has been given authority and power over absolutely everything in the world, including the president of the United States and the nation itself, including the king of England and the empire he rules, including all governments, all corporations/ businesses, all schools, all neighborhoods, all families, absolutely everything.

The lordship of Jesus is crucial, because it means that . . .

1.) **When we surrender our lives to his lordship, to his rule in our lives, we align ourselves with the deepest truth of our world**. When we surrender our lives to him, we take our proper place as his servants, as his followers in the worldwide, universe-wide kingdom of the most powerful ruler there ever was or ever will be.

2.) The lordship of Jesus is profoundly good news! The God who created and sustains our world is good, loving, and merciful. If Jesus really is the supreme Lord over all things, that means that **love and goodness and mercy are the fundamental principles of our world and of our future**. It means that love and goodness are the most important realities now and will win in the end. We can live in joyful confidence knowing that the God who is loving and good and merciful will be the one to determine the final outcome of the human project.

That may be why we all seem to love happy endings, why we get choked up by stories of heroism, noble sacrifice, and self-sacrificing love. We respond with deep feeling, because those stories echo or retell the deepest truth about the world in which Jesus really is Lord over absolutely everything! They remind us that selfishness and cruelty and evil are not the deepest truths of our world, and that sin and death are being destroyed and will someday be finally destroyed.

3.) **As the people of God, we have nothing to fear from any earthly ruler, authority, power**. They might be able to make our lives easier or more difficult, they may hassle us, they may even take our things or even our lives, but they cannot ultimately destroy us. Nothing they do can separate us from the love or the power of God if Jesus is Lord.

4.) If Jesus really is Lord, then that means **he is (still) using his authority and his power to call followers, to heal bodies, to cast out demons, and to forgive sins**. It means he has authority over absolutely *everything* in your life and my life, even the really big things that worry us and that tie us up in knots.

That gives us profound confidence, faith, joy, peace, and hope. As followers of our Lord Jesus Christ, we have access to a power far greater than the power of any government, any economy, any powerful people, any powerful influences/ habits/ addictions, than the power of our bodies or the power of our past.

The first four implications listed above are widely embraced by Christians in many denominations. The additional implications listed below are particularly important to Anabaptists.

5.) **Jesus is Lord of Scripture.** When you look at the world around you, the lenses you look through affect what you see, they change how you see things. Changing lenses changes your perspective. For example, cameras can be fitted with a standard lens (focusing much the way your eye does on something in front of you), a telephoto lens (bringing distant objects closer and reducing the distance between the foreground and the background), a wide-angle lens (pulling a wider view into the frame than a standard lens), or a fish-eye lens (a super wide-angle lens). Each will produce a very different photo from the others. The lens you use shapes how you see and understand what you are looking at.

The lenses in the glasses I wear help me to see the world around me more clearly. I'm nearsighted, so without the help of the lenses in my glasses, everything more than about three feet away from me is some amount of blurry. In other words, I see things very differently depending on whether or not I'm looking through my glasses. When we say that people who are overly optimistic are "looking through rose-colored glasses," we mean that most things look brighter and sunnier to them than they do to anyone who isn't seeing the world through "rose colored lenses."

Anabaptists interpret Scripture through a "Jesus lens." We interpret Scripture in light of the lordship of Jesus over all things, including the interpretation and application of Scripture. In other words, as the *Confession of Faith* says,

> we seek to understand and interpret Scripture in harmony with Jesus Christ as we are led by the Holy Spirit in the church. . . . Because Jesus Christ is the word become flesh, Scripture as a whole has its center and fulfillment in him. (*COF* 1995, 21-22)

We approach Scripture this way in obedience to the example and instruction of Jesus, who claimed the authority to interpret Scripture properly. You can see this clearly in the Matthew 5 "You have heard that it was said ... but I tell you ... " statements.

For example, in verse 38 when Jesus says, "You have heard that it was said, 'Eye for eye, and tooth for tooth,'" he isn't just reminding them of a general proverb. He is quoting Moses, the one who spoke for God and through whom God's law was given. This instruction is part of the fabric of their way of life. In its time, it called for God's people to live by a higher standard than their neighbors, because it limited their response to the harm done to them. It was more typical then, and still is today, to want to do even more damage to the person who harmed me than the harm I received, both to pay the person back and to deter them in the future. Of course, in practice, that just escalates the trouble when my enemy responds in kind.

Jesus goes on to call his followers to an even higher standard than the standard given through Moses.

> You have heard that it was said, ... But I tell you, do not resist an evil person. If anyone slaps you on the right cheek, turn to them the other cheek also. And if anyone wants to sue you and take your shirt, hand over your coat as well. If anyone forces you to go one mile, go with them two miles. Give to the one who asks you, and do not turn away from the one who wants to borrow from you. (Matt. 5:38-42)

Scholars debate what Jesus meant with these instructions, mainly whether he is calling us to simply withstand or to actively resist our opponent through nonviolent means. My point here is that whatever specifics he had in mind, he is clearly exercising the authority to reinterpret Scripture and to call his followers to a higher standard than the one previously in place. If you have any doubt about that, read the immediately preceding verses in Matthew 5:43-47, where Jesus calls us to love our enemies!

Jesus was also very clear that he and his purpose were the whole point and the fulfillment of all of what the Scriptures have to say. To the Jewish leaders he said,

You study the Scriptures diligently because you think that in them you have eternal life. **These are the very Scriptures that testify about me,** yet you refuse to come to me to have life (John 5:39-40). To his disciples, he said, " 'Everything must be fulfilled that is **written about me in the Law of Moses, the Prophets and the Psalms.' Then he opened their minds so they could understand the Scriptures.**" (Luke 24:44-45)

In other words, Jesus gave them a new understanding of the Scriptures they had been reading and memorizing all their lives. According to Jesus himself, they needed to interpret the Scriptures through a "Jesus lens" to understand them properly.

The gospel of John says that Jesus is also our key to better understanding God. "No one has ever seen God, but **the one and only Son**, who is himself God and is in closest relationship with the Father, **has made him known**" (John 1:18). The Greek translated "made him known" has the sense of explaining or expounding in great detail, so other English translations say Jesus "revealed" or "declared" or "explained" God.

The writer of Hebrews tell us that Jesus, the Living Word, is the preeminent revelation of the will and character and nature of God, fulfilling and superseding the Written Word (the Scriptures), when he says that

> In the past God spoke to our ancestors through the prophets at many times and in various ways, **but in these last days he has spoken to us by his Son**, whom he appointed heir of all things, and through whom also he made the universe. The Son is the radiance of God's glory **and the exact representation of his being**, sustaining all things by his powerful word. After he had provided purification for sins, he sat down at the right hand of the Majesty in heaven. (Heb. 1:1-3)

Notice that the writer also repeats the phrase we mentioned earlier—sitting at the right hand of God—to remind his readers of the lordship of Jesus.

Our goal, as New Testament followers of Jesus, is to understand the teachings of Jesus and his apostles, and beyond that the entirety of the Scriptures, as a whole and as they were intended by God. We consider the life, teachings, example, death, resurrection, and lordship of Jesus to be essential to understanding the Bible as a whole, so we are very intentional about reading and interpreting Scripture "through the Jesus lens." We refer to this as a "Christocentric" or Christ-centered way to read and interpret Scripture.

We interpret such Scriptures to mean that God is most fully and most clearly revealed in Jesus, that Jesus gives us the best and most complete picture we have of the character and nature of God, and that every other picture or idea we have about who God is or what God is like needs to be adjusted to align with the representation of God we see in Jesus. We believe God revealed his character, his nature, and his purposes more and more clearly over the centuries of human history until his revelation culminated in Jesus. We call this "progressive revelation."

That doesn't mean that every single verse or even every story or chapter specifically mentions Jesus or that it has him specifically in mind. It *does* mean that, in order for you to understand everything you read truly, you need to understand how the text you are reading fits into the larger story of God's work to redeem the world in and through Jesus. Some material is in the background, some is in the foreground, some is at the periphery, some is at the center, but the central defining reality toward which and toward whom it all points is the person, life, teachings, and work of Jesus Christ.

We agree with Christian Smith (a Roman Catholic sociologist), as far as he goes, when he writes,

> From the Bible's account of the creation of the world in Genesis to its final consummation in Revelation, it is all and only about the work of God in time and space in the person of Jesus Christ for the redemption of the world. (Smith 2012, 98)

So, when Anabaptists wrestle with theological or ethical matters, our starting point is to ask questions like, Are the conclusions we come to about God, about how to live our lives, about how to treat other people consistent with what we know about how Jesus lived? Are they consistent with his teachings about how we should live? Are our conclusions consistent with the significance and meaning of his death, his resurrection, and his ascension? Is our approach to the events and teachings of the Old Testament consistent with these considerations?

This also means that whenever we seek to answer the moral and ethical challenges of our time, including questions about sex or sexuality, creation, identity, evolution, warfare, or social media, we begin by asking, "What, if anything, did Jesus say or do about this?" or "How does this relate to who Jesus was and what he said?" or "Did Jesus embrace this or reject this?"

6.) **Jesus is central to all of what God is doing in the world**. Westerners are used to thinking of the spiritual world and the material, physical world as separate realities, but that way of thinking would have been foreign to the authors of the Scriptures. These authors do distinguish between the seen and unseen worlds, between the temporal and the eternal worlds, between heaven and earth, but both of these worlds or realities are considered part of God's creation. In their minds, there's constant movement and close interaction between the two.

The mission of God encompasses all aspects of the spiritual and material worlds, and the New Testament presents Jesus as the center and focal point of all of what God has done, is doing, and will do in these worlds. The poetry of John's Revelation refers to Jesus as "the first and the last" and "the beginning and the end" (Rev. 22:13). In other words, Jesus is somehow the key to all human history, making no distinction between spiritual and physical realms. It all began in and through him, and it will all end in and through him (Wright 2016).

The poetic imagery of Revelation 5 tells the same story. In this dramatic scene, set in God's throne room in heaven, no one other than "the Lion of the tribe of Judah, the Lamb who was slain"—Jesus—is worthy to open (that is, to fulfill) the scroll of the redemptive plan of God in human history. No one else has the standing or the capacity for this task, no one else is worthy of it, other than the one who has accomplished the victory of God over sin and death through his suffering, death, and resurrection.

Paul says this more concretely in Colossians 1 in his soaring hymn of praise, beginning in verse 15. He says that Jesus (the Son) is the one through whom all things were created. All things. Everything that is seen and everything that is unseen whether in heaven or on earth. He is before and above all things, and in some way we don't fully understand, "in him all things hold together." The coherence of the world we live in depends on Jesus. Without his sustaining presence or power, the world as we know it would come to an end.

> The Son is the image of the invisible God, the firstborn over all creation. For in him all things were created: things in heaven and on earth, visible and invisible, whether thrones or powers or rulers or authorities; all things have been created through him and for him. He is before all things, and in him all things hold together. (Col. 1:15-17)

He goes on to say in verse 18 that God meant for Jesus to be supreme in everything, including in his project of setting all things right. It's through Jesus that God is reconciling and will reconcile all things to himself (to his original purposes), including everything that is seen and everything that is unseen. All things will be set right through the work of Jesus.

> And he is the head of the body, the church; he is the beginning and the firstborn from among the dead, so that in everything he might have the supremacy. For **God was pleased** to have all his fullness dwell in him, and through him **to reconcile to himself all things, whether things on earth or things in heaven, by making peace through his blood**, shed on the cross. (Col. 1:18-20)

That means that nothing God has done, is doing, or will do in human history or in all of world history has been accomplished or will be accomplished except through Jesus. The mission of Jesus' on earth is just part of the bigger picture of God's engagement with his creation project, but Jesus' mission on earth was and is central to all of what God had in mind for that project.

7.) **Jesus is Lord over everything in our lives.** Jesus calls us to acknowledge and surrender to his lordship. He calls us not only to acknowledge that he is Lord, but to yield to him, to cooperate with him, to surrender to him. He calls us to align our lives with the truth of who is really in charge.

When we surrender to his lordship, we welcome his rule over every area of our lives. There is nothing in our lives that's not subject to his authority. That means that we attempt to align everything we do with our minds, all the parts of our bodies, our money, our time, our talents, our work, our power (or influence), and our relationships with Jesus' teachings and example.

We will have much more to say about this in chapter 5, but we will simply note here that just as the lordship of Jesus extends to everything in all of creation, so too his lordship extends to every corner of our lives. He calls us to an ongoing way of life, a faith that's lived out. He is asking for far more than just a brief expression of regret for our sins. According to the New Testament, when I surrender my life to Jesus, nothing listed in the paragraph above is really mine any more. Everything on that list, and anything else we could have listed, belongs to Jesus, for him to use or direct as he pleases.

8.) **Our allegiance to Jesus is more important than any other allegiance.** If Jesus is truly Lord of absolutely everything, then our allegiance to him outranks, comes before, and supersedes any other commitment we might make. Every other allegiance we have needs to be evaluated or judged by who Jesus is and what he calls us to do. All of our commitments need to be reconsidered and reshaped to make sure they align with our surrender to Jesus.

Our allegiance to Jesus should never be compromised or weakened or undermined in any way by our allegiance to anyone or to anything else. Nothing and no one else comes anywhere close to him in terms of its true authority. Nothing else should have a stronger impact on how we think, what we do, or how we live our lives than our surrender to Jesus, including our allegiances to our clubs, our families, our employers, our tribes, or our nations.

We who have pledged allegiance to Jesus may deeply love and even sacrificially serve in or through any of these groups, but we can never do or say anything motivated by our loyalty to these groups that would contradict our allegiance to him. Nothing any of these groups asks us to do or say or believe is more important than what Jesus calls me to do or say or believe.

Summary

Underlying all the beliefs and practices of the Anabaptist approach to following Jesus is the core belief that Jesus is Lord over absolutely everything. When Paul expands on Jesus' simple statement that "all authority in heaven and on earth has been given to me," he says that Jesus is now

> **far above any ruler or authority or power or leader or anything else**—not only in this world but also in the world to come. **God has put all things under the authority of Christ** and has made him head over all things. (Eph. 1:21-22 NLT)

If that's really true, it changes everything. If we are convinced of this truth, then its implications will ripple out to shape every part of our lives, every part of who we are, and everything about who we hope to become. In this chapter, we reviewed eight implications of this reality, but all the other core beliefs and practices presented in the following chapters are also implications of the supreme lordship of Jesus. This whole book and the entirety of Anabaptist life and thought can be seen as a multifaceted finishing of the phrase, "If Jesus really is Lord of absolutely everything," then . . .

I hope it has been profoundly encouraging to you to be reminded that Jesus
- really is ruling over all other authorities and all other powers,
- is able to rule in your life and in the world around you, and
- has the authority and the power to bring all things to their proper end and he will do so.

I challenge you to surrender your life and all of who you are to the lordship of the resurrected and ascended Christ. I urge you to carry this phrase with you into your day as a one-sentence reminder prayer, "Jesus is Lord of absolutely everything." Ponder what it means and how it might change your life to embrace its reality deeply.

NOTE: You can read more about the themes covered in this chapter in the following articles of the Confession of Faith in a Mennonite Perspective—*2: Jesus Christ, 10: The church in mission, 21: Christian stewardship, and 24: The reign of God*

Chapter 3

The Kingdom of God Is Where People Unite Under the Lordship of Jesus

Core belief 2: The Kingdom of God

What images or associations come to mind for you when you think about the word *utopia*? I don't hear it often in my conversations, but for me it brings to mind harmony, happiness, justice, and flourishing shared by everyone. It turns out the word was first used more than 500 years ago in the title of a fictional story about travel to an island of plenty and equality, written by Sir Thomas More. Since then, many people have thought and written about what utopia would look like.

The idea of the perfect human society has fired the imaginations of philosophers, political scientists, sociologists, science fiction writers, novelists, and artists. Since no one claims that we currently live in a utopia, most of their work is focused on how to achieve it. They envision ways to get there, ways we could make progress toward a better future.

In the early 1980s, artist Robert McCall was commissioned to paint a picture that would express the hope and the promise of a better future that would inspire visitors to Disney's new EPCOT Center (EPCOT stands for Experimental Prototype

Community of Tomorrow) which opened in 1982. The futuristic mural he painted is called "The Prologue and the Promise." The light in the painting is very bright, and the scene weaves together advanced technology, harmony with nature (lots of green), and harmony among people of many nations. This huge painting is bursting with beauty, abundance, light, and vivid color.

We all have some sense of wanting our lives to be or to look something like that, with harmony and peace radiating out in all directions. The key question is, How would we get there? How could we move toward that better future? Most of the answers we get today have nothing to do with God. Most of the answers don't see God's presence or God's work as important or good. Most of the answers rely on some combination of new technology, good or improved government, eliminating all the bad guys, producing more sustainable energy or agriculture, or devising just and fair economic arrangements.

McCall painted a secular picture of a hopeful future for Disney's EPCOT Center, but does any of it look familiar to you? Do you see echoes of ancient pictures of flourishing from the Bible? Like the Garden of Eden in Genesis? Or the peaceable kingdom in Isaiah 11? Or the picture of heaven in the book of Revelation?

Karl Marx was an influential author in the modern study of human societies. He wrote during the Industrial Revolution in Europe (mid-1800s), when obscenely wealthy owners of mines and factories treated the miners and factory workers like a renewable energy source (as raw material for their enterprises) rather than like human beings. The workers were dramatically overworked and vastly underpaid. While they lived in deplorable conditions, the business owners lived in luxury.

Marx saw injustice and exploitation all around him. He condemned the injustice and called for the whole system to be upended. In its place, Marx imagined an ideal human society (a utopia) where every person had plenty to eat, where all had control over their work and income, where people's basic needs were met, where every person was treated justly and with dignity, and where everyone could live at peace.

It was also important to him that any notion of God be removed from this utopia, because he saw the church as part of the problem of how people were being mistreated. To Marx, the church seemed to bless the system that was grinding people down and seemed to be focused on making sure the workers accepted their fate.

Of course in most cases the movements Marx called for and inspired have created the opposite of the utopia he had in mind. His proposals for how to achieve a better future have caused as much or more misery than he witnessed during the Industrial Revolution. But that's for another discussion.

What always struck me about Marx's picture of the ideal human society was how similar it seemed to be to heaven or to Jesus' picture of the kingdom of God. I was amazed by how much Marx's ideal human society seemed to be inspired by the ideals of the Christian story. I think it's fair to say that, according to those ideals, if God's reign extended fully in the world, every person would have plenty to eat, everyone would have at least some control over their work and income, everyone's basic needs would be met, everyone would be treated justly and with dignity, and everyone would live at peace.

The main difference for Marx was that he imagined human beings could create their own ideal society—a heaven-like society—by intentionally excluding God. Keep in mind that he considered churches a huge part of the problem, because they seemed to be focused on persuading people to accept their misery as part of God's plan for the world.

On the other hand, according to the story the biblical authors tell, the presence of God and the rule of God are *the* foci of the ideal human society. That story tells us that human beings were created to live in relationship with God, to always be oriented toward the person, the character, and the nature of God. If that's true, then no human society that's focused on anyone or anything else will be perfect or ideal.

The primary disaster in the biblical story is that sin entered the created world almost immediately in the way the creation story is told. Sin is any action or way of thinking that contradicts or rejects the nature or character of God. Sin disrupts the mission of God in the world. The more we sin by contradicting or rejecting God and his purposes, the more power we give sin to shape our thoughts and our actions. The further we walk down that path, the more entangled we become in sinful habits and the farther we find ourselves from God. Despite the exciting rewards sin promises to provide, we find that it actually produces turmoil, brokenness, and destruction. If we continue to persist in the face of the destruction sin creates, we will eventually find ourselves very far from God and discover that this path ends with spiritual death.

In most printed Bibles, sin starts breaking things on page 3 of a book that's over 1100 pages long! As a result, we know very little about what the created world and human life were like before that. We know that it was very good, that human beings were created in the image of God himself, that God was immediately present with them, and that all their needs were met, but that's about it. The ideal human society, the harmony of the earth was apparently wrecked almost from the beginning.

The reason this was such a disaster is that the action of **disobeying God broke four key relationships** that will not be fully restored until God brings all things in the created world to their proper end (Hershberger 2013, 22). Because of its far reaching consequences, Scot McKnight says sin is "hyper-relational." (McKnight 2007, 23). The advent of sin in the story broke....

1.) The relationship **between Adam and Eve and God**. When Adam and Eve disobeyed God (Gen. 3), it meant they didn't fully trust God. Think about that for a moment. They had immediate, personal contact with the God who created them. They spoke directly with him, and yet somehow they turned away from him almost immediately in the way the story is told in Genesis. We don't have any way to know for sure exactly how much time elapsed between their creation and their first sin, but we know that when they disobeyed, they were separated (cut off) from him by their sin, and their relationship with God was never the same.

That separation between us (human beings) and God has persisted ever since. The idea that human beings would not trust their good and loving creator who made them in his own image to reflect him in the world is incredible to consider. And yet, people through the centuries, including many today, repeat this same mistake. The first relationship sin wrecked was our individual and collective relationship with God.

2.) Their relationship **with each other**. When Adam and Eve disobeyed God, they almost immediately turned on each other. Eve blamed the serpent, but Adam said it was Eve's fault. Adam and Eve expressed a lack of trust in each other, a break in their relationship of loving trust and intimacy. They passed that lack of trust on to their children. In the very next chapter of the story (Gen. 4), their son Cain kills his brother Abel. It's incredible to me how near the beginning of the story of the created world this happens. Not only can they not fully trust each other, but we have the first intentional killing. They were separated (cut off) from each other by suspicion, envy, and mistrust. The second relationship sin wrecked was our relationship with each other.

3.) Their relationships **with themselves**. Once they disobeyed God, Adam and Eve understood evil from their own experience. They were aware they had chosen evil rather than good and were stuck with the aftermath of a decision they could not undo. Now they understood God's warning that their "eyes would be opened" if they disobeyed his instruction. They were no longer innocent of what evil was and their own decision to embrace it rather than trusting God's guidance for them.

It's interesting that the account in Genesis doesn't include any expressions of remorse from Adam or Eve. We know that they hid from God in fear, and we have their statements of blame, but nothing else. Whatever they may have felt in the initial encounter with God after disobeying him or when they were banished from the Garden, they knew from experience that they could no longer trust themselves to do what was right. Ever after, they would suspect their own motives and actions. As their heirs, we know how tormented we can be by guilt, shame, and despair in the wake of our own choices to sin. The third relationship sin wrecked was our relationship with ourselves.

4.) Their relationship **with the created world**. One consequence of their disobedience was that Adam and Eve were permanently removed from their intended home in the Garden of Eden. Another was that the ground was cursed as part of God's judgment on their sin. Ever since, the ground has resisted our efforts to produce crops, requiring "painful toil" and "the sweat of your brow." If you have ever tried to grow food crops, you may wonder with me how amazing effortless farming would have been. Can you imagine what it would be like to raise food crops without hard labor, without weeds, and without sweat? I would love to experience that some day!

Human beings were included in the created world to represent God in and to the world. God intended for them to rule as loving, benevolent caretakers in much the way God would if he could somehow be physically present within the creation himself. Creating human beings was a way for his nature and character to be expressed in the created world.

But when his representatives disobeyed him, that part of the project was twisted. The purpose for including them in the created world was undermined. People still had the capacity to do incredible good, but they then realized that they also had the capacity to do incredible evil and harm. The loving, benevolent care of the rest of creation they began to provide in Genesis 2 had been permanently disrupted. The fourth relationship sin wrecked was our relationship with the created world.

Reconciliation Is the Heart of the Gospel Message

The most incredible and amazing good news is that God began to promise from the very moment of Adam and Eve's disobedience to repair and to restore each of these four relationships. God took it on himself from the earliest days of human history to reestablish these relationships and the ideal human society where harmony and beauty are flowing in all directions. All he asks is that we cooperate with him.

The Hebrew Scriptures use the word *shalom* to describe the reality that God intends to restore in the created world. It's usually translated "peace" in English, but the meaning of the Hebrew word is much broader and richer than the usual meaning of the English word. We experience "shalom" when things are whole or complete, when we are able to relax because everything is as it should be. Shalom includes full well-being, flourishing, justice, and loving relationships. Full shalom means all four of the broken relationships have been restored, so that harmony is flowing in all directions. It refers to all of life, the entire created world, being restored to the way God intended it to be.

Anabaptists believe that the primary goal of God's work in and through Jesus, is to restore all things in the created world to himself, that in and through Jesus God began to set everything right that was broken or destroyed when humankind (in Adam and Eve) disobeyed God and invited sin to start breaking things. We believe that reconciliation—the restoration of the four broken relationships and the restoration of shalom in its fullest sense—is the heart of the good news Jesus came to announce.

We get this from Paul, who says it very clearly in Colossians 1. He begins by reminding us of the supreme lordship of Jesus (where we began our list of core beliefs) in verses 15-18.

> The Son is the image of the invisible God, the firstborn over all creation. For in him all things were created: things in heaven and on earth, visible and invisible, whether thrones or powers or rulers or authorities; all things have been created through him and for him. He is before all things, and in him all things hold together. And he is the head of the body, the church; he is the beginning and the firstborn from among the dead, **so that in everything he might have the supremacy**. (Col. 1:15-18)

He then goes on to say that the gospel he proclaims to everyone who will listen is that "God is reconciling ***all things*** to himself through the obedience of Jesus."

> For **God was pleased** to have all his fullness dwell in him, and through him **to reconcile to himself all things, whether things on earth or things in heaven, by making peace through his blood**, shed on the cross. Once you were alienated from God and were enemies in your minds because of your evil behavior. **But now he has reconciled you by Christ's physical body through death** to present you holy in

his sight, without blemish and free from accusation—if you continue in your faith, established and firm, and do not move from the hope held out in the gospel. This is the gospel that you heard and that has been proclaimed to every creature under heaven, and of which I, Paul, have become a servant. (Col. 1:19-23)

He says something similar, but more succinctly, in Ephesians 1 when he writes,

With all wisdom and understanding, he [God] made known to us **the mystery of his will** according to his good pleasure, which he purposed in Christ, to be put into effect when the times reach their fulfillment—**to bring unity to all things in heaven and on earth under Christ**. (Eph. 1:9-10)

In other words, it's only in light of the death, resurrection, and ascension of Jesus that we understand that all along God's plan was to bring unity to all things under Christ. It turns out that God's purpose all along was to restore the shalom he intended for the whole created world from the beginning through the person and work and obedience of Jesus. Through Jesus, God has begun the process of reconciling all things to himself, that is, of properly aligning them with himself and with his original intent for how all things would fit together.

It is through the obedience and sacrificial death of Jesus on the cross that God provides forgiveness for our sins, releases us from the bondage sin has woven around us, and breaks the power sin has over our hearts and minds. This fulfills the promise the angel made to Joseph before Jesus was born when he said, "[Mary] will give birth to a son, and you are to give him the name Jesus, because he will save his people from their sins" (Matt. 1:21).

Jesus was very aware of this aspect of his earthly mission. At his last meal with his disciples before his death, he "took a cup, and when he had given thanks, he gave it to them, saying, 'Drink from it, all of you. This is my blood of the covenant, which is poured out for many for the forgiveness of sins'" (Matt. 26:27-28).

Of course, as wonderful and as amazing as it is, the forgiveness of our sins is not the whole story of our salvation. Because our sins and the power of sin together represent the primary barrier to the flourishing of human society, removing that barrier through the sacrifice of Jesus makes reconciliation possible. The full salvation God has in mind for us includes restoring the full flourishing of human society and the full flourishing of everything God created in the beginning.

As the four broken relationships are repaired, the kingdom of God is reestablished on the earth. Because the death of Jesus makes possible a whole new way of living, his apostles gratefully and joyfully refer to Jesus throughout their writings in the New Testament as our "Savior" (Acts 5:31, Acts 13:23, 2 Timothy 1:9-10) and as "our Lord and Savior" (2 Pet. 1:11, 2:20, 3:2, 3:18).

Reconciliation in Jesus Repairs All Four Broken Relationships

1.) The relationship **between us and God**. In Romans 5:6-11, Paul describes our reconciliation to God through the death of Jesus, which is the restoration of the first broken relationship. The Greek word translated "reconciliation" in verse 11 means "the reestablishment of an interrupted or broken relationship." In Ephesians 3:12, he assures us that "in [Christ] and through faith in him we may approach God with freedom and confidence."

2.) Our relationships **with each other**. Jesus' main command to his disciples in John 15 is "Love one another as I have loved you." He says they will remain in him by obeying that commandment. In Ephesians 2:13-23 Paul reminds his readers that in Christ, God has destroyed the barrier of hostility separating Jews from Gentiles, and they are now all one people in whom God is dwelling. In Galatians 3:28 he extends this point when he says that in Christ there's also no barrier between slaves and free people or between men and women. We are all one in Christ Jesus. The second broken relationship—our relationship with each other—has also been restored.

3.) Our relationships **with ourselves**. The repair of the first two relationships spills over into the repair of the third, giving us peace with ourselves or peace within ourselves. Through the work of Jesus, we have been released from guilt and shame and despair. God the Holy Spirit restores our ability to say no to sin, and we can approach God with freedom and confidence as his dearly beloved children.

We receive the blessing Jesus gave his disciples when he said, "Peace I leave with you; my peace I give you. I do not give to you as the world gives. Do not let your hearts be troubled and do not be afraid" (John 14:27). Paul also reminds us that we can now live in peace with ourselves because we have been reconciled to God. "Do not be anxious about anything, but in every situation, by prayer and petition, with thanksgiving, present your requests to God. And the peace of God, which transcends all understanding, will guard your hearts and your minds in Christ Jesus" (Phil. 4:6-7).

4.) Our relationship *with the created world*. Our collective relationship with the created world is the one of the four that's furthest from full restoration. In Christ, we can see God's good creation through his eyes—as an intricate, beautiful, and abundant treasure for us to enjoy, enrich, and care for well. The people of God understand that "the earth is the Lord's" and that we have been entrusted with it as caretakers.

Paul reminds us that God's work of reconciling all things to himself extends to the entire created world when he says, "the creation itself" is still groaning as it waits to "be liberated from its bondage to decay and brought into the freedom and glory of the children of God" (Rom. 8:19-22). The promise in Revelation 21 is that this will entail a new heaven and a new earth. Not only will God return to dwell with his people again (as in the beginning in the Garden of Eden), but he also announces, "Look, I am making all things new!" (Rev. 21:5 CEV). Everything in the whole created world will get a fresh start when God restores all things to the way they ought to be, when he aligns everything with his original intent, when he restores full shalom.

American evangelical presentations of "the gospel" often limit the presentation to the restoration of two of the four relationships—our personal relationship with God (peace with God), mainly so we can be assured of "getting into heaven," and our relationship with ourselves (peace within). It's an over-individualized version of the gospel that suits American individualism. To put it crudely, too many of us truly believe that God's main focus is on how I'm doing now and what my future will be.

While it's true that the gospel promises the restoration of these two relationships, that's only the beginning rather than the end of the matter. The larger and more important reason we are reconciled to God is so that we can then take our proper place in the kingdom that God is forming right now. Being reconciled to God frees us to live with each other and in the created world in the way he intended us to live in the beginning. For someone living out reconciliation in all four relationships, the afterlife is simply a continuation of the project that begins now (Hershberger 2013, 115; McKnight 2007, 61, 75, 119).

Some have suggested that a call to peace with each other and peace with the whole created world are optional extras or additions to the gospel of Jesus proclaimed. Unfortunately that way of thinking overlooks Jesus' own emphasis on the central importance of the kingdom of God and betrays a limited understanding of the scope of God's work in the world.

The Kingdom of God Is Where People Unite Under the Lordship of Jesus

The good news Jesus came to announce was that the kingdom of God has now come, that the time has finally come for God to begin restoring the four relationships and the ideal human society where harmony and beauty are flowing in all directions. He said, in my paraphrase, "Come and be a part of living out the shalom of God as it begins to expand in the world!"

Jesus called his followers to join together as a new community that would live out the reality of the shalom of God in their daily life together (Bender 1944, 36). Their reconciliation with God made it possible for them to be reconciled with each other. Their new identity as children of God would be shared with anyone who surrendered to the lordship of Jesus and who was reconciled to God. They would treat each other with dignity and respect, loving each other from the heart, and serving each other as though they were all part of the same birth family.

In a new sense, they *were* all part of the same birth family, because they were all "born again" into the family of Jesus followers. So they were now brothers and sisters to each other regardless of how rich or poor they were, regardless of whether they were slave or free, Jew or Gentile, male or female, and regardless of their nationality or ethnicity. In the U.S. today, this means that Jesus followers are not separated from each other by being white or black or Hispanic, rich or poor, Republican or Democrat or libertarian, American or any other nationality. It was then and is today a mind-blowing idea that, in Christ, we will truly love and care for each other as family despite these kinds of barriers that continue to separate people so rigidly in the societies in which we live.

It turns out that our restored relationships with each other as followers of Jesus bring about a whole new society, just as he said they would. God is calling people to be part of his re-creation project from every family, every people group, people living in every nation of the earth so that all the people of the earth will eventually come to honor God, both in their worship and in their life together.

In Revelation 5, John describes a worship gathering in heaven, celebrating the reconciliation Jesus has made possible among all the peoples of the earth.

> Then I saw a Lamb, looking as if it had been slain, standing at the center of the throne, encircled by the four living creatures and the elders.... And they sang a new song, saying: "You are worthy to take the scroll and to open its seals, because you were slain, and **with your blood you bought for God persons from every tribe and language and people and nation. You have made them to be a kingdom and priests to serve our God, and they will reign on the earth.**" (Rev. 5:6,9,10)

As N. T. Wright sometimes puts it, our life together now is meant to be a "working model" of the kingdom of God that will one day fill the entire created order. Or as Ron Sider put it,

Jesus' gospel includes the fact that the messianic reign has in fact begun and there is now a reconciled and reconciling community whose visible life is a powerful sign of the kingdom that has already begun and will someday arrive in its fullness. (Sider 1999, 76)

Many of us have already experienced some of this reality even if it isn't yet fully realized. There are many stories in Christian biographies of former enemies embracing each other as brothers and sisters once they surrendered their lives to Jesus. People who once hated or feared each other find out that their enemy has also surrendered their life to Jesus, and they are now a brother or sister in Christ. The former enemies now have a closer bond than the one they share with their birth family or with people from their nation of origin.

Here is one such example. You may recall that Japan invaded mainland China in 1931 and committed a series of horrible atrocities there up until and during World War 2. A Japanese navy pilot in World War 2 named Takashi Yamada flew missions against China and the U.S. during the war. The one mission he declined to carry out was a kamikaze (suicide) mission to crash his plane into a U.S. Navy ship. After the war, Yamada became a Christian believer, was baptized, and eventually became a pastor and church leader in Japan.

Many years later, Yamada was in Taiwan, meeting with some Chinese Christians. A Chinese man who had once fought against the Japanese invaders offered his hand to Yamada and said, "We were once enemies of each other, but now we are brothers in Christ."

Yamada says he was humbled to the point of tears to know that someone his people had so badly mistreated was acknowledging their peoplehood, their unity in Christ. He says he understood in a new way "the higher spiritual solidarity in Christ [that goes beyond] our racial and cultural solidarity. The church is a community of God's people surpassing their racial, national, and cultural human ties" (Freeman 1999, 367).

We will say more about Christian community in the Anabaptist understanding of Christian faith in chapter 6.

God Invites Us to Join God's Mission of Reconciliation

It's incredible good news that in Christ we can be reconciled with other followers of Jesus, enjoying a whole new way of living together. But God also invites us to join him in extending reconciliation and peace beyond the Christian community, out into the world around us. That means that, as a sign that we are being transformed by the power of the Holy Spirit at work in our lives, we will find ourselves cooperating with, being kind to, making sacrifices for, and loving people who are not followers of Jesus. The Holy Spirit will even enable us to love and serve people we might reasonably be expected to be arguing and fighting with, people we are struggling to trust, and people we have no obvious reason to care about.

Paul says this clearly in 2 Corinthians 5. Too often we lift verse 17 (see below) out of its context to focus on the individual impact of surrendering our lives to Christ. Of course, that's part of the amazing good news Jesus makes possible, but it's about much more than individual salvation or transformation. Our reconciliation with God is one small part of God's project of reconciling the entire world to himself in Christ.

As if that were not enough, God has entrusted you and me with the ministry of reconciliation. He sends us out into the world as agents of reconciliation, sharing in the work he is doing. Dallas Willard (who was not an Anabaptist) got right to the uncomfortable heart of the matter when he said the main test for Christ-like character is whether we spontaneously respond to our enemies with love (Wilder 2009, 3).

> Therefore, if anyone is in Christ, the new creation has come: The old has gone, the new is here! All this is from God, who reconciled us to himself through Christ and **gave us the ministry of reconciliation**: that **God was reconciling the world to himself in Christ**, not counting people's sins against them. And he has **committed to us the message of reconciliation**. We are therefore Christ's ambassadors, as though God were making his appeal through us. We implore you on

Christ's behalf: Be reconciled to God. God made him who had no sin to be sin for us, so that in him we might become the righteousness of God. (2 Cor. 5:17-21)

Peter also reminds us that communities of Jesus followers have a priestly function in and to the world. In other words, part of our call is to represent God to the world and to represent the world to God. The world around us should be able to see God in us (among us) and to hear what God has to say through us. God should be able to see the world as it should be in us (among us) and to receive proper worship through what we say and through how we live.

> As you come to him, the living Stone—rejected by humans but chosen by God and precious to him—you also, like living stones, are being built into a spiritual house to be **a holy priesthood**, offering spiritual sacrifices acceptable to God through Jesus Christ. . . . **[For] you are a chosen people, a royal priesthood, a holy nation, God's special possession, that you may declare the praises of him who called you out of darkness into his wonderful light.** Once you were not a people, but now you are the people of God; once you had not received mercy, but now you have received mercy. (1 Pet. 2:4-5, 9-10)

The early Anabaptists believed that everyone should hear the call of Jesus and have the opportunity to respond to it. Everyone should have the opportunity to choose to become a follower of Jesus. They further believed that choosing to follow Jesus included a commitment to help to carry out the great commission. For them, part of following Jesus was calling others around them to repent, believe the good news, and join in following as well. So every member was considered a potential preacher and missionary (Schaeufele, 1962).

So again we say, your salvation is about far more than just making sure you end up in heaven! Your surrender to the lordship of Jesus is just beginning of you being joined to the people of God *and* to us serving together as a holy and priestly community to all the people groups around us. Your reconciliation with

God, your salvation means you are joining God's re-creation project of making all things new. He is re-creating heaven on earth among us. Of course, Jesus never claimed that the kingdom of God was fully present. He taught that it's already present, even if not yet complete. His kingdom won't be fully present on earth until he comes again and finally completes what he began in his first coming.

Several years ago, God taught me more about this than I wanted to learn when we lived near a difficult neighbor. When we moved in, we had a sense of God placing us in this neighborhood not just to live our lives there but to love our neighbors actively. Some of them were Christian believers but others were not.

Sometime later, "Ben" moved into the area. Ben was very smart and had lots of interesting stories and ideas to share but also had shouting matches with some of the neighbors within months of moving in.

In the years Ben lived among us, his encounters with neighbors sometimes ended badly. He would be friendly and chatty until they crossed him, and then *boom!* He would unleash profanity and insults . . . and they would have nothing more to do with him.

Eventually that happened to me. Like everyone else, I wanted to avoid Ben's explosions, but the Holy Spirit would not let me just ignore him. It was partly that he lived close enough that we would keep crossing paths. It just didn't feel right to remain permanently hostile to and cut off from him when I had accepted the challenge of actively loving my actual neighbors.

Over time, I learned to let the moment of the explosion pass, avoid meaningful contact for weeks or even months, and then approach Ben again with kindness. Not weakness, but kindness . . . and patience and grace. He and I were usually able to find our way back to a working relationship again, at least for a time, and even though I was not entirely sorry when he moved away, I was able to wish him well and really mean it when I said goodbye to him.

Being Agents of Reconciliation Means We Are Peacemakers Rather Than Peacekeepers

As Jesus said in Matthew 5:9, "Blessed are the peacemakers, for they will be called children of God." In his reflection on this verse, Dietrich Bonhoeffer wrote [note: I have changed "them/they/their" to "us/we/our"],

> The followers of Jesus have been called to peace. When he called us we found our peace, for he is our peace. But now we are told [by Jesus in Matthew 5:9] that we must not only have peace but make it.
>
> His disciples keep the peace [make peace?] by choosing to endure suffering ourselves rather than inflict it on others. We maintain fellowship where others would break it off. We renounce all self-assertion, and quietly suffer in the face of hatred and wrong. In so doing we overcome evil with good, and establish the peace of God amid a world of war and hate.
>
> But nowhere will that peace be more manifest than where we meet the wicked in peace and are ready to suffer at their hands. The peacemakers will carry the cross with our Lord, for it was on the cross that peace was made. Now that we are partners in Christ's work of reconciliation, we are called the sons of God as he is the Son of God. (Bonhoeffer 1963, 126)

As I said, I learned more about how to be this kind of peacemaker than I wanted to by living next door to Ben. I learned to step away from his verbal blasts rather than respond in the moment, let some time pass, pray, wait, take a deep breath, reset, and then reengage. I learned that between my encounters with him it was important to . . .

- assume the best about him, not rage against him in my mind;
- avoid gossip about him with my wife, my children, or our neighbors;
- resolve which matters I needed to bring up with him and which matters I could just forgive and let go.

I embraced these lessons not because I was weak or because

I enjoyed being verbally insulted or humiliated, but because I came to believe God the Holy Spirit wanted to teach me more about kindness, patience, perseverance, and mercy through this relationship. I believed he wanted me to learn to experience peace in the face of conflict and turmoil. I was also determined not to let Ben's behavior define who I was. I didn't want to give in to bitterness, rage, insults, or gossip. I simply did not want to become that kind of person. That would have been the far easier (and weaker) path to follow! It was much harder to become a peacemaker.

Somehow, over several years, I came to love Ben (a sure sign of the Holy Spirit at work!), not with mushy affection but with respect for his journey and the troubles that had wounded him. I actually felt compassion for him, because I had come to see that he was trapped by his habits, imprisoned by his insecurities, and rarely able to trust other people deeply. He was a troubled and unhappy person whose behavior isolated him from the people around him. I eventually realized that his outbursts were doing more harm to him than to me. There's a part of me that's glad I learned these lessons from my connection to Ben, but I was also relieved when the lessons ended with his moving out of the neighborhood.

Citizens of Two Kingdoms

God is far more patient than you are or I am. I don't think either of us would be willing to let the solution to the destruction caused by sin unfold in bits and pieces over thousands of years. And yet in his wisdom and patience, that's exactly what God has done. Even when Jesus came proclaiming the arrival of the kingdom of God, he did so in humility and hiddenness rather than in overwhelming power. He said the kingdom of God would begin to impact the world (the kingdom of the world) in the way yeast impacts dough—starting very small, growing slowly, but having a significant impact in time.

That means you and I live in an in-between time. We live in the era between two major Jesus events—between his first coming and his second coming. His first coming marked the launch of the kingdom of God on the earth, but it didn't displace the kingdom (or the kingdoms) of the world where other powers and rulers and authorities are in charge. Jesus and his apostles tell us that will not happen until Jesus comes again to complete the restoration of all things.

So, based on what Jesus taught, we believe the kingdom of God is now fully present in the world but also isn't complete. The full reality of the kingdom of God, that is, the universal lived experience of the lordship of Jesus, will not become obvious until Jesus returns to the earth in a visible, physical way.

That means you and I will be citizens of two kingdoms until Jesus' second coming. We are citizens of the kingdom of the world (a nation state is one particular kingdom of the world), and when we surrender our lives to Jesus, we become citizens of the kingdom of God. Followers of Jesus have wrestled with this reality since the time of his first coming. We wrestle with the sometimes competing and sometimes overlapping requirements of these two kingdoms. Jesus' disciples wrestled with this tension even while he was with them.

Anabaptists point out that Jesus and his apostles say almost nothing about what the kingdoms of the world should do. His primary focus was on what citizens of the kingdom of God should do. Jesus had very little to say about the major issue confronting the Jewish people of his time: How should we (How does God want us to) respond to the Roman Empire and to its domination of all aspects of our life? He focused almost all of his time and energy on talking about what the kingdom of God is like and how to respond to his call to "follow me."

A very insightful and helpful discussion of these issues as they apply in the United States is Greg Boyd's *The Myth of a Christian Nation* (2005). The book details how beliefs and practices of "the kingdom of the cross" differ from those of "the kingdom of the sword" from a New Testament perspective. An adaptation of a sermon series, the books addresses a host of very practical issues we confront when considering how God may or may not be at work through national governments in what Boyd calls "the kingdoms of the world" (the nations of the world).

At the very least, if the kingdom of God is where people unite under the lordship of Jesus, it seems that we should see a clear distinction between the way communities of Christians live together and the way communities of non-Christians live together. Among other things, we would expect a much higher standard of relational harmony in communities of Christians. We would not expect the same amount of reconciliation and peace to be possible in the kingdom of the world, among people not committed to walking in the way of Jesus.

Another tension we live with as citizens of two kingdoms is that the kingdom of God unites the followers of Jesus across ethnic and national boundaries, that is, it unites people who live in different kingdoms of the world. In our world today that means our brothers and sisters in Christ may be from different ethnic groups than ours or may live in different nation states than ours, but the kingdom of God should not be confused with any one kingdom of the world. So what do we do when the interests or policies of my ethnic group or nation state conflict with those of the ethnic group or nation state of my brothers and sisters? Of course, we stand with our brothers and sisters in Christ, but that's not always simple or easy when political or military tensions pit us against each other.

In 2007 and 2008, Christians in Kenya struggled with this exact tension as presidential politics pitted two coalitions led by rival ethnic groups against each other, both of which the Joshua Project estimates to be ninety-eight percent Christian. One coalition was led by the Kikuyus and the other was led by the Luos. When the results of the election were disputed, two months of armed violence followed. Hundreds of people were killed, and an estimated 600,000 people were displaced.

The tie to their ethnic groups was so powerful that some Christians took up arms against their brothers and sisters in Christ. The Christians who stood together across the ethnic divide opened themselves to charges of betraying their families in a cultural setting were people live with a much stronger collective mindset than Westerners do.

Of course, Westerners live with the same tension and have struggled for centuries, often unsuccessfully, with the temptation to believe that my commitment to my nation or to my ethnic group is more important than my commitment to love and serve my brothers and sisters in Christ who happen to be from another nation or ethnic group.

One of the most shocking aspects of World War 1 was the fact that the various nations of Europe who considered themselves Christian nations carried out an unimaginably brutal war against each other. The people of each nation saw themselves as doing God's work in conducting this war. One highly respected German theologian even announced that the German army was the earthly means God would use to usher in the kingdom of Christ.

World War 1 was the first large-scale war that used machinery to kill people in far greater numbers, so the "Christian" nations of the world ended up killing millions of each other's soldiers, often in horrific ways. Citizens of each nation demonized the soldiers of the other nations but considered their own soldiers martyrs and saints (Jenkins 2014, 104). Opponents of the war, regardless of their reasons, were often considered unpatriotic and a shameful threat to their own nation. It was hard to hold on to the perspective that Christians should not be pitted against each other for kingdom-of-the-world reasons in such a tense and highly charged atmosphere.

Primary Allegiance to Jesus Christ

For followers of Jesus, that is, for those who have surrendered themselves to the lordship of Jesus, there's no other allegiance that's more important than our allegiance to him. There's no other kingdom or nation or ruler or authority or commitment whose pronouncements or requirements take priority over the commandments and requirements of Jesus or of the kingdom of God. Every other allegiance we embrace needs to be limited by our allegiance to Jesus Christ. If we are surrendered to the lordship of Jesus, whenever another authority asks us to do or say something that doesn't fit with Jesus' teachings, we need to refuse to comply.

The practical challenge is that our daily lives are filled with thoughts and words and actions that are shaped by our allegiances and our commitments. In fact, it's hard to imagine any thoughts or words or actions that are not in some way shaped by our allegiances. That means it's vital for us to remember that no other allegiance or commitment is more important than my primary allegiance to Jesus Christ. It means that my commitments to my family, my marriage, my children, my tribe, my people group, my town, my nation, my employer, my possessions, my church, my financial goals, my job, my career, my ambitions, and my hobbies all need to be surrendered to my allegiance to Jesus.

Summary

Our second core belief flows from the first, which is that Jesus is Lord over absolutely everything. If that's true, then the kingdom of God is simply the place where people unite under the lordship of Jesus. Jesus' mission in coming to live among humankind as one of us was to make this kingdom possible and to release it into the world.

The first coming of Jesus and all it included was a major fulfillment of God's longstanding promise to repair the four relationships that were broken soon after creation. The restoration of our relationship with God makes possible the restoration of our relationships with each other and a whole new way of living together. In our newly restored relationships with each other, we live out Jesus' great command to his disciples to "Love each other as I have loved you."

We will not be able to do this perfectly until he fully reconciles all things to himself, but because the kingdom of God really has already come, we see the people of God already expanding to include people from every tribe, every language, every people, and every nation on the earth. Our bonds to each other in the kingdom of God are deeper than any earthly bonds as we live out God's call to be a reconciled and reconciling community. Jesus promised that the proclaimed and lived reality of this community would permeate the world as transformative good news.

This community is open to anyone willing to surrender to the lordship of Jesus and to join us in the mission God has given us to live out this way of life. Some have suggested that reconciliation and peacemaking are optional extras that weigh down or interfere with the gospel of individual salvation, but the mission of God in the world is about far more than just the forgiveness of your or my sins. The mission of God is to reconcile all things in the whole creation to himself through the person and work of Jesus Christ. The kingdom of God is where people unite under the lordship of Jesus.

NOTE: You can read more about the themes covered in this chapter in the following articles of the Confession of Faith in a Mennonite Perspective—*5: Creation and divine providence, 6: The creation and calling of human beings, 9: The church of Jesus Christ, 10: The church in Mission, 22: Peace, Justice, and Nonresistance, 23: The church's relation to government and society, and 24: The reign of God.*

Chapter 4

We Choose to Follow Jesus

Core belief 3: Choose

My grandmother's name was Lucinda. She was always "Grandma" to me, but other people knew her as Lucinda. When I met Grandma's friends or visited her church with her, people thought they knew me at least a little bit because they knew I was Lucinda's grandson. I didn't mind. I loved her and respected who she was. She was quiet, steady, warm, and she liked to laugh. I was happy to be known as her grandson. And now, after what seems like only a few years, I'm a grandparent myself! And, if you know me and then you meet *my* grandchildren, you think you know them at least a little bit because you know they are my grandchildren.

But guess what. I didn't choose my grandmother. I was just born into her family. We loved each other dearly, but she didn't choose me out of a pool of potential grandsons, and I didn't choose her out of a pool of potential grandmas. My grandchildren didn't choose me to be their grandpa either. They were just born into our family. We know this is how it works, so it might seem a little strange even to think about choosing your grandparents. That is, unless you don't have any. In that case, you might look for and choose someone to fill that role in your life.

Maybe you have heard the phrase "God doesn't have any grandchildren." That phrase is true, because becoming part of

God's family works differently from the way we become part of our biological families. We don't choose to become part of our biological families, but we have to choose to become part of God's family.

A central part of the good news Jesus came to announce is that through his life, death, and resurrection, we can be saved from the power and penalty of sin, and we can begin to live a whole new way of life as the children of God—regardless of whose children we have been before. We can be reconciled to God and live as his children. It really is true that no matter who you are or what you have done, you can choose to become a child of God and a citizen of the kingdom of God.

The gospel of Mark says that after Jesus was tempted in the desert, he

> went into Galilee, proclaiming the good news of God. "The time has come," he said. "The kingdom of God has come near. **Repent and believe the good news!**" As Jesus walked beside the Sea of Galilee, he saw Simon and his brother Andrew casting a net into the lake, for they were fishermen. "**Come, follow me,**" Jesus said, "and I will send you out to fish for people." At once they left their nets and followed him. (Mark 1:14-18)

Jesus called people of all sorts to follow him. Over and over he said, "Follow me." Some people did what Simon and Andrew did here. Many people followed him, but many did not. This is still the call of Jesus to you and to me—repent, believe the good news, and come, follow me.

Repent

We don't use the word *repent* very much anymore. It's now mostly used by Christians, and we often assume it means to feel remorse or regret for wrongdoing. We are mostly focused on how someone feels about their sin. In the New Testament, repentance is more something you do than something you feel. For Jesus and his disciples, repenting means you turn away from sin and you turn to God. You change directions. You stop walking away from God and begin walking toward God (Camp 2003, 72).

That's why Paul says he preached the same message to both Jews and Gentiles, "I preached that they should repent and turn to God and demonstrate their repentance by their deeds" (Acts 26:20). In other words, if your repentance is genuine, people around you will notice real changes in your behavior. Sorrow or remorse may lead you to repent, but the key is that you actually change directions. In 2 Corinthians 7:10 Paul says godly sorrow *produces* repentance.

When Jesus calls people to repent, his focus seems to be both on turning away from sin and on turning away from trusting in rule-keeping to please God. He calls us to trust that we really can become the children of God and please him by faith (believe this good news) and, on that basis, to change directions (repent) and begin living the way of life Jesus both calls us to live and enables us to live.

Peter echoed this call on the day of Pentecost when he said, "Repent and be baptized, every one of you, in the name of Jesus Christ for the forgiveness of your sins. And you will receive the gift of the Holy Spirit. The promise is for you and your children and for all who are far off—for all whom the Lord our God will call" (Acts 2:38-39).

Many years later, Menno Simons wrote,

> Therefore, we exhort you with Christ Jesus, believe the gospel, that is, believe the joyful news of divine grace through Jesus Christ. Cease from sin; manifest repentance for your past lives; submit obediently to the Word and will of the Lord; and you will become companions, citizens, children, and heirs of the new and heavenly Jerusalem, free from your enemies, hell, death, sin and the devil, if only you walk according to the Spirit and not according to the flesh. (Simons 1539, 116)

In this one brief quote, Simons touches on several important Anabaptist themes: Repent (change your behavior), (choose to) believe, turn away from sin, submit (turn to God) in obedience, take your place among the people of God, relying on the power of Holy Spirit.

Choosing to Believe

In his gospel, John refers to "believing in him" over and over. At the end of the book of John, he says I wrote out this account of Jesus' life so that you would "believe that Jesus is the Messiah, [that he is] the Son of God, and that by believing [in him] you may have life in his name" (John 20:31). In other words, I wrote this account to convince you of this.

Jesus himself talks about believing in him or trusting that what he is saying is true. For example, in John chapter 3, Jesus uses this phrase five times:

> Just as Moses lifted up the snake in the wilderness, so the Son of man must be lifted up, that everyone who **believes** may have eternal life in him. For God so loved the world that he gave his one and only Son, that whoever **believes** in him shall not perish but have eternal life. For God did not send his Son into the world to condemn the world, but to save the world through him. Whoever **believes** in him is not condemned, but whoever does not **believe** stands condemned already because they have not **believed** in the name of God's one and only Son. (John 3:14-18)

The clear assumption running through this passage is that everyone is able to believe or not believe. No one is so lost or so corrupted or so far from God that they lose the capacity to make this choice. Jesus also talks about the decision to believe as something everyone resolves for themselves, something they resolve freely and without coercion. Each of us either believes or we don't believe.

Jesus was clearly disappointed to see that some of the people who encountered him in person, who heard his teachings, and who saw the miracles he performed still did not believe. You can hear this when he says, "You have seen me and still you do not believe" (John 6:36). Even so, he didn't compel them to believe. He didn't deceive or manipulate or badger them. He let them decide.

Jesus invites us, he urges us, he commands us to believe in him, to follow him, to obey him, but he doesn't force anyone to accept his invitation or obey his command. No one else can force you to believe in him either. No one can make you obey his commands or force you to follow him. No one can accept his offer of true life and forgiveness for you. No one can believe or follow for you. The invitation from Jesus is an offer you have to choose to accept for yourself.

In the time of the early Anabaptists, in the 1520s, if you were born in what we now know as Spain, you would have been considered Catholic because your king was Catholic. A very common way to produce more Catholics was to conquer more territory so the kingdom of a Catholic king could include more people who would then be considered Christian. If you were born in many parts of what we now know as Germany, you would have been considered Protestant because your ruler (usually a prince) was Protestant.

In those days, to be a citizen in good standing with your community, you would have been expected to believe certain things about God and about how to live for God based on where you lived. You would have been expected to worship in a particular way because of the choices made by your king or your prince—whoever's rule you were under.

That probably seems strange to you, especially if you grew up in the United States. Americans are used to living in a country that includes "freedom of religion" as a core ideal. We understand that to mean we have freedom of choice regarding religious commitments. The idea that a ruler or the government would tell us what to believe or how to worship seems foreign to us.

The early Anabaptists were some of the first to argue that rulers and governments have no business directing the religious beliefs and practices of their subjects. They based their stance on the New Testament, on the example and teachings of Jesus and his apostles, who made clear that the lordship of Jesus and the claims of the kingdom of God supersede the authority and the claims of any of world's kingdoms. Jesus clearly intended for his followers to treat his teachings and his commands as more important than the directives of the religious and political leaders of his time. The Anabaptists sought to restore that approach in the life of the Christian community.

Anabaptists also believe that even God himself will not make this choice for you and doesn't decide who will believe and who will not believe. The sense of Jesus' statements from John 3 is that this is a decision God has entrusted to us despite the risk this entails. God has gone to great lengths, at great cost to himself, to be reconciled with us, but God doesn't force us to accept the offer to be reconciled to him.

God freely offers reconciliation with himself and full citizenship in the kingdom of God to anyone who will repent, believe the good news, and follow Jesus. In John 3:16, Jesus says that **whoever** believes in him will not perish but have eternal life. In John 6:40, he says that's God's will "is that **everyone** who looks to the Son and believes in him shall have eternal life." Peter also writes later, "[The Lord] is patient with you, not wanting **anyone** to perish, but **everyone** to come to repentance" (2 Pet. 3:9).

There are Scripture passages in the New Testament (see John 6:37, 6:44, Rom. 8:29-30) that seem to refer to God choosing us rather than us choosing him. These seem to limit God's offer to be reconciled and our ability to respond to it to those whom God has chosen. Paul even introduces the term "predestined" to describe the children of God in Romans 8 and Ephesians 1. There's clearly some tension here with the broad scope of God's will as just described. You can see the two themes interwoven without a clear resolution in Jesus' comments in John 6.

Since we believe Jesus is the Lord of Scripture, Anabaptists address this tension by considering it within the whole framework of Jesus' teaching. We ask, What all did Jesus have to say about who chooses whom?

For example, one important factor in trusting that God welcomes everyone to choose freely is that that's exactly what Jesus did. He extended his call to everyone who would give him a hearing, and he let them make up their own minds. For example, at the end of John 6 after Jesus shocked his listeners by telling them they could not be his disciples if they were unwilling to eat his flesh and drink his blood (you and I would have been shocked, too), verse 66 says, "From this time many of his disciples turned back and no longer followed him."

Jesus let them walk away, even though he must have known that some of them thought he meant they would be required to eat his actual flesh and drink his actual blood. Even though they were disciples rather than casual listeners, and even though there were many of them, Jesus didn't run after them offering to sort out the misunderstanding. He let them make their own choices.

Another example is his disciple Judas Iscariot. Judas lived and walked closely with Jesus throughout his ministry. We don't know what internal battles he fought with belief and unbelief, but he believed enough to be chosen by Jesus and to be counted among his disciples. In the end, his unbelief was profound enough that he betrayed Jesus, and Jesus let him choose to do so. We have no indication that Jesus interfered in any way with Judas's eventual choice, even though the consequences of that choice would be catastrophic for Jesus.

I'll say more about this in Chapter 5, but we should also keep in mind that we live in a very individualistic age. Westerners tend to assume that God's main focus is on his relationships with individuals rather than on his relationship with his people as a whole. We tend to read the Bible as though it was written mainly to and for individuals. It's very hard for us to consider that verses describing God choosing or predestining or electing may actually refer to him determining that there will be *a people* who follow him without assuming that he also chooses *the individuals* who will follow him.

In other words, one way to resolve the tension about who chooses whom is to see God's choice as corporate (we has decided that he will work through the people of God). At the same time, God allows full freedom to individuals to choose whether or not to be part of the people of God.

You may think that the choices you have made in the past have ruined your chances with God. You may worry that you are so far from God, so lost in sin or brokenness that his offer of reconciliation through Jesus has been canceled in your case. Maybe you just feel unworthy of such mercy and forgiveness. But Jesus says **whoever** believes is welcome, and Peter reminds us that it's not God's will that **anyone** should be lost in sin and brokenness. We believe that Jesus' example shows us that no one is ever so ruined by sin that they are unable to respond to Jesus' command to "repent, believe the good news, and follow me."

The truth is that none of us is good enough on our own, no matter how careful we have been. None of us is or ever will be worthy on our own. We are all hopeless without the mercy and love of God, which is about who God is and not about who you or I are. John 1:12 says that anyone who believes in him is given the right to become a child of God. All who believe (for themselves) are given the privilege of being fully reconciled to God and welcomed into the family of God. That's what we mean when we say God doesn't have any grandchildren. Only children.

The Challenge of Consumerism

But this whole idea of "choosing" is a little tricky for us, especially for Americans and other Westerners. We are very used to making choices as consumers. We are used to picking the products and the entertainment and even the people that please us and to rejecting the ones that don't. We are so used to making choices about so many aspects of our lives that we have begun to think the world around us should always be reshaped to please us, and we don't even realize this is happening.

That means it's very easy for me to begin thinking of Jesus as just another choice for *me* to make. It's very natural for me to think that I'm inviting Jesus into *my* world, into *my* experience. I can even think of Jesus as just another tool or product or person that might be useful to me or helpful to me in shaping the life I want to live. That's the challenge consumerism presents when we talk about choosing to follow Jesus.

It's true that Jesus promises us abundant life. He promises us forgiveness, mercy, joy, and peace. You are probably thinking, Wow! Yes, please! *But* what we often overlook, what we don't want to think about very hard is that *God* is the one who gets to define what those good gifts look like. We tend to assume that God's goal for us is the same goal we have for ourselves, which is mostly to live comfortable lives that impress the people around us. Unfortunately that's not true. God's goal is for us to look more and more like Jesus as we live and serve together with our brothers and sisters in Christ. Following Jesus will likely require us to do things that are very uncomfortable for us, and there will likely be times when the people around us look down on us.

Listen to what Jesus said about how much it would cost us to choose to follow him. One time

> A large crowd was following Jesus. He turned around and said to them, "If you want to be my disciple, you must hate everyone else by comparison—your father and mother, wife and children, brothers and sisters—yes, even your own life. Otherwise, you cannot be my disciple. And **if you do not carry your own cross and follow me, you cannot be my disciple.**
>
> **"But don't begin until you count the cost.** For who would begin construction of a building without first calculating the cost to see if there is enough money to finish it? Otherwise, you might complete only the foundation before running out of money, and then everyone would laugh at you. They would say, 'There's the person who started that building and couldn't afford to finish it!' . . . So **you cannot become my disciple without giving up everything you own**. (Luke 14:25-30, 33, NLT)

It's clear that Jesus doesn't see himself or his way as a tool we use to become more successful or more popular or healthier or richer. He isn't offering to be useful to us for the main purpose of accomplishing *our* goals. On the contrary, he calls us to "die to" or to fully break our reliance on everything we counted on before surrendering to him and beginning to follow him. Truly following Jesus means trusting that he knows what is good for me better than I do and better than the people around me do. "Dying to ourselves" includes giving up being in charge of deciding what is best for us. Jesus invites us to give that up rather than holding on to it.

Jesus speaks from the perspective of the one who is Lord over absolutely everything. He lovingly commands us, he invites us, he urges us to do what he knows is best for us, which is to surrender fully to him, to give up everything else. In essence, he is saying, "Don't choose to follow me unless you are serious about it, unless you are willing to value following me over absolutely everything else." Here in Luke 14, he says you need to value following me over your family ties, your own life, and your comfort (a cross is an instrument of humiliation, torture, and death). In other places, he says you need to value following me over your possessions, your money, your popularity, and (again) your comfort.

Writing in his context shaped more than seventy years ago, British author C. S. Lewis described his experience of yielding to God's priorities in his life:

> When a man turns to Christ and seems to be getting on pretty well (in the sense that some of his bad habits are now corrected) he often feels that it would now be natural if things went fairly smoothly. When troubles come along—illnesses, money troubles, new kinds of temptation—he is disappointed. These things, he feels, might have been necessary to rouse him and make him repent in his bad old days; but why now? Because God is forcing him on, or up, to a higher level: putting him into situations where he will have to be very much braver, or more patient, or more loving, than he ever dreamed of being before. It seems to us all unnecessary: but that is because we have not yet had the slightest notion of the tremendous thing He means to make of us.
>
> Imagine yourself as a living house. God comes in to rebuild that house. At first, perhaps, you can understand what He is doing. He is getting the drains right and stopping the leaks in the roof and so on: you knew that those jobs needed doing and so you are not surprised. But presently He starts knocking the house about in a way that hurts abominably and does not seem to make sense. What on Earth is He up to? The explanation is that He is building quite a different house from the one you thought of—throwing out a new wing here, putting on an extra floor there, running up towers, mak-

ing courtyards. You thought you were going to be made into a decent little cottage: but He is building a palace. He intends to come and live in it Himself. (Lewis 1952, 174)

Here's how this is working out in the life of a friend of ours, an insightful young woman who experienced a miscarriage when she was eight weeks pregnant with her second child and who gave me pemission to share some of her journey. At first she thought, "'Oh no big deal—eight weeks is pretty early for a miscarriage. It happens. You can always try again.' But several weeks later, a grief set in, a grief deep in my core. I felt like something was missing. After that, nothing could shake the grief that kept crawling back into my mind and heart.

"And I started wrestling with God. Asking him to just take the feeling away, to end the grieving process. I wanted to move on so badly. I eventually realized that I was severely discontented in large part because *my* plans for my life had been disrupted. I wanted things that no longer seemed possible. I wanted my babies to grow up close in age, to make the empty room in our house a well-loved and used space, and I wanted a family of five before I turned thirty-five (preferably earlier). That was 'my plan/dream' for myself, for our family, and up until recently, we were on track to see it come true. Part of what I was grieving was the loss of that dream.

"As I continued to pray and grieve and ponder, I realized how much I had been given and that God knew what I needed. If you had asked me in high school what I would be doing at age 30, my dreams would not have been focused on family life. High-School-Me would have told you that at thirty I would be single, driving a Volkswagen Beetle, working in a biological warfare defense program in a big city with a cat at home.

"But when I gave my life to God, he did something entirely different with it. I didn't want and resisted every single one of the things that have brought the greatest joys to my life because they weren't in 'my' plan. Although there has been immense pain with each of these blessings God has given me (because God doesn't promise ease), I have a husband who challenges me and loves me better than I could have ever imagined, a son who brings light to every room he is in, a job as an anesthesiologist that is fulfilling, and the richest experience of all, a relationship with God that is continually growing deeper.

"So now, despite what I'm missing, I am content. I understand what Paul meant when he wrote, 'And the peace of God, which surpasses all understanding, will guard your hearts and your minds in Christ Jesus.' In realizing how God has shaped my life, I hear him say, 'I know what I'm doing, where you are going, and I am enough.' And my soul responds with a sigh of relief."

Our friend has counted the cost and continues to choose to follow Jesus faithfully. She is living out what it means for her to "die to her self." She is being richly blessed, but she has also experienced "immense pain with each of the blessings" she has received as the Holy Spirit has begun to transform her so that she is thinking and living and looking more and more like Jesus.

Implications/What It Means

For Anabaptists, when "we choose to follow Jesus," when we choose to follow the one who is Lord over absolutely everything, we understand that to mean that we accept his rule over us, too. It means that we are choosing to surrender to, to cooperate with his direction for absolutely every part of our lives. Choosing to follow Jesus means surrendering to his way.

As we have seen, this is a costly choice. It's a choice that, according to Jesus, should be taken seriously, since even though it's free, it costs us everything. This isn't just a simple consumer choice between self-help products. It's not just intellectual assent to a set of abstract beliefs (Camp 2003, 103-104).

It's a whole life, lifelong surrender to a way of living that will, at least sometimes, put us at odds with the people around us. But it's also a wholehearted embrace of the one who knows us best and who loves us the most. It's a wholehearted devotion to a person (Jesus) and to a way of life that provides profound peace and hope and joy that don't depend on our circumstances. Following Jesus provides us with a foretaste of what life will be like in the age to come.

Anabaptists understand all of this to mean that . . .

1. Conversion is the starting point of a life of discipleship. It's not the end goal of our spiritual quest. Your choice to surrender to Jesus and to begin following him is a profoundly meaningful and joyful moment to celebrate in your life. It's the portal through which you step into the life of the age to come, into the kingdom of God, as a child of God and as a part of the family of God. It's the beginning of the process of being transformed into the likeness of Jesus.

This was a particular point of emphasis for the early Anabaptists, because they were dismayed at how little people's everyday lives seemed to be impacted by being Christians. Catholic Christianity seemed to be more about observing rituals than about seeing changed lives. The Christianity of the other reformers seemed overly focused on correcting doctrine and an overly spiritualized and internal experience of conversion.

The Anabaptists understood Jesus and his apostles to teach that a true inner conversion will be evident in the way someone lives their life. A genuine inner conversion will inevitably be expressed outwardly in behavior changes everyone can see. In fact, according to historian Arnold Snyder,

> Anabaptists soon gained a reputation for being sober, upright and honest people. There were actually several cases of people arrested on suspicion of being Anabaptists simply because they had stopped cursing, gambling and getting drunk. They were not released from jail until they had proven that their turn for the better had nothing to do with joining the Anabaptists. (Snyder 1999, 29. Also see Bender 1944, 25)

2. God's response to a sincere decision to repent and believe the good news was not only to forgive our sins but also to baptize us with his Spirit. God the Holy Spirit comes to live within us when we choose to surrender to the lordship of Jesus. The Holy Spirit is the one who, by his presence and power at work in our lives, begins and then continues the process of regeneration—the process of transformation into the likeness of Jesus. This isn't something we can accomplish on our own. It can only hap-

pen by the power of the Holy Spirit at work within us. But it's also true that someone who is genuinely converted can't avoid being changed in noticeable ways when the Holy Spirit is at work within them.

That's why Anabaptists have always insisted, as we will see in chapter 5, that a changed life (or perhaps a changing life) is essential evidence of one's conversion. Teaching that one can be truly converted without any impact on one's life or character would be to deny the presence or the power of the Holy Spirit.

Some authors have called the early Anabaptists the evangelists or the evangelicals of the Reformation because of their emphasis on the importance of conversion. Others have called them the charismatics of the Reformation because of their emphasis on the importance of the presence, power, work, and guidance of the Holy Spirit. Of course, over time, their emphasis settled on the fruit of the Spirit's work rather than what later came to be called the signs or the gifts of the Spirit's work.

3. Water baptism is the external sign of the person's inner baptism with the spirit. It's the outward physical announcement that someone has chosen to repent, believe, and follow. The inner baptism (with the Spirit) is primary and essential. The outer baptism (with water) is just the public announcement of the inner baptism (Snyder, 1999, 25). In other words, we baptize believers, people who have chosen to follow Jesus. When we're baptized, it mean's we're old enough to make our own decision to follow Jesus and have freely and voluntarily chosen to do so.

4. We celebrate the choice of a young child to follow Jesus, but we don't baptize young children. We believe that children are innocent before God until they are old enough to make a meaningful whole life, lifelong commitment that may cost them everything, including their lives. We don't believe infants are born bearing the guilt of sin which can only be resolved by a baptism that they have no way of choosing or refusing. Infants and young children are not capable of responding to Jesus' call to repent, believe, and follow in the way he describes in Luke 14.

(Note: Mennonite leaders and congregations vary in how they apply this understanding. Where they have been impacted by an emphasis on conversion as a simple but crucial individ-

ual decision, they have baptized younger and younger children. Congregations influenced by an evangelical concern for "child evangelism" have baptized children as young as five or six and don't usually emphasize "joining the church" as part of what baptism means.)

Among more conservative Anabaptist groups, like the Amish, people are usually not baptized until they are ready to join the church as adults, often in their early twenties. In such groups, joining the church means embracing a very distinctive pattern of life that prescribes, among other things, specific ways of how you dress, run a business, transport yourself, communicate with other people, and use technology.

It's more typical for young people in Mennonite congregations to be baptized sometime between ages twelve and eighteen, depending on their level of maturity, understanding, and sincerity. By that time their choice to follow Jesus can be less about pleasing their parents and other adults and more fully based on their own understanding and voluntary surrender. They will also have a clearer picture of the social and moral cost of following Jesus than young children can have.

Summary

Our third core belief cannot be separated from the first two. We *choose* to follow Jesus—the one who is Lord over absolutely everything. This isn't a choice that anyone can be forced to make, nor can anyone else choose for you. God has enough authority and power that he could have made this decision for you, but he has decided not to. He invites anyone and everyone to respond to his loving initiative by choosing to follow him freely and voluntarily.

When we choose to follow Jesus, we become part of and are united to the worldwide group of people, of brothers and sisters, who have also chosen to follow Jesus. We become part of the kingdom of God, which is the place where people of every tribe and nation and people group are united in and by our surrender to the lordship of Jesus.

We will say more about this in the next chapter, but we have also seen that choosing to follow Jesus means surrendering to his way. This involves far more than just an internal mental or spiritual exercise. The call of Jesus is to "repent, believe the good news, and follow me."

There's no way to do these things as Jesus intended if we approach them flippantly. They are far-reaching, life-changing commitments. Following Jesus means living a different life than we would have lived if we were not surrendered to his lordship. That's why he said, Count the cost before you decide!

With all that in mind, I urge you to do what Jesus calls all of us to do: repent, believe the good news of the kingdom of God, and begin following him.

If you have already done this, I urge you to keep following. I urge you to continue to grow in your understanding of what that means in your life.

I urge you to surrender more and more of your life to him whenever you discover any part of your life that isn't yet fully surrendered to him.

I also urge you to ponder your honest answers to the following questions:

Are you trusting that Jesus knows what's good (best) for you even better than you do?

Are you trusting that his love for you is going to care for you even more profoundly than your love for yourself?

Are you trusting that his love for you will reshape you to be more like him and that that will be a good thing, even if his renovations hurt sometimes?

If you have never chosen to follow Jesus, if you have never fully surrendered to his rule in your life, I urge you to do so today. I hope you understand more of what that means after reading this chapter and are feeling drawn to do this.

Come join the worldwide gathering of the children of God who are on this journey. Come join us on this adventure of following our loving and gracious Lord who gives us all we need, but who also asks us to surrender everything to him. Come take your place in the ever-expanding kingdom of God.

NOTE: You can read more about the themes covered in this chapter in the following articles of the Confession of Faith in a Mennonite Perspective—*6: The creation and calling of human beings, 7: Sin, 8: Salvation, 9: The church of Jesus Christ, 11: Baptism, and 18: Christian spirituality.*

Chapter 5

We Follow Jesus in Everyday Life

Core belief 4: Follow

When I was a teenager, bell-bottomed pants were very cool. At least I thought they were. That might be hard for you to imagine now, but I bought it wholeheartedly. My favorite pair of jeans, until I wore them out, had flares at the bottom that were large enough to cover the entire length of my feet. It was a sad day for me when I finally had to part with them. I also really wanted to grow shoulder-length hair, but my hair just grew bushier when it was long rather than reaching down toward my shoulders. I remember being pleased at how unique and counter-cultural I was in those years.

But when I got to college and began to understand the insights of sociology, I realized that while I was dressed differently from many adults around me, almost none of my ideas for how to do that were original. In all the ways I thought I was being uniquely counter-cultural, I was just modeling myself after a different group of people. All my ideas for how to be "unique" came from outside of myself. I didn't think up any of them on my own. Several years later, I laughed out loud with understanding when I saw a bumper sticker that read, "You are unique! Just like everyone else." That's still one of my favorite phrases.

The reality is that we are social beings. That means that all of our ideas about who we are, how the world works, and what's good or bad come from our interactions with other people. If we had no one to react to us, no one to reflect back to us what they see in or expect from us, we would quickly be lost and disoriented. We are always conforming to or trying to live up to the standards and expectations of some group of people or trying to live in contrast to those standards and expectations.

In Christian terms, we would say humans all "worship" something or someone outside ourselves. That is, we all focus our attention on, dream about, take our cues from, make sacrifices for, and spend time and money on something or someone external to us. It's just part of how we are wired as human beings. We are all devoting time, energy, and enthusiasm to something beyond ourselves. We can't choose not to worship, but we can choose what or whom we worship. In everyday language, we might say, we are all passionately following something or someone outside ourselves, so choose carefully what or whom you follow.

Christians believe we are wired to worship God as part of how we were created by him. In other words, we were created to live our lives in loving relationship with God. We were created to devote our primary time, energy, and enthusiasm to our connection to the God who is love. Because of who God is and who we are in relation to him, the appropriate framing of our relationship with him is worship. As we saw in chapter 4, God has given us the freedom to choose whether or not our worship will be devoted to him. Sadly, as we saw in chapter 3, that relationship was broken by sin very early in the story of God's creation project. Ever since that initial fall into sin, our inclination has been to resist worshiping God, even though that's what we were created for.

The insight that we are wired for worship is doubly important because of what James K. A. Smith points out in the title of his book *You Are What You Love* (Smith 2016). Smith explains that not only are we oriented to something outside ourselves, but over time we will become more and more like whatever or whomever we are devoted to. In short, we become what we love. If that's true, it's vital to choose the focus of our devotion carefully, because in choosing what or whom to worship, we are also choosing who we will become.

We looked at quite a few Scriptures in chapter 4 that highlight Jesus' call to repent and believe. Our focus in that chapter was on the importance of *choosing* to repent and believe. But most of those Scriptures include a third command also repeated frequently in chapter 4: "Follow me." This third command is our focus here. We *follow* Jesus in our everyday lives.

As we saw in chapter 4, after Jesus was tempted in the desert, he

> went into Galilee, proclaiming the good news of God. "The time has come," he said. "The kingdom of God has come near. **Repent and believe the good news!**" As Jesus walked beside the Sea of Galilee, he saw Simon and his brother Andrew casting a net into the lake, for they were fishermen. "**Come, follow me,**" Jesus said, "and I will send you out to fish for people." At once they left their nets and followed him. (Mark 1:14-18)

Jesus repeated these three commands over and over in his preaching—repent, believe the good news, and come, follow me. He clearly tells the crowds that you can't claim to be his disciple if you aren't following him. For example, in Luke 14:27 he says, "If you do not carry your own cross and follow me, you cannot be my disciple." In New Testament terms, a disciple is an apprentice, someone who learns from a master how to be like the master.

Disciples seek to understand their master, but not just so they can grasp what and why their master says what he says and does what he does. They seek to understand deeply so that they can model their own thinking and speaking and living after the patterns provided by their master. That's the way in which we are called to follow Jesus. Disciples of Jesus seek to reflect his mindset, his nature, his character in how we live our lives.

Anabaptists understand Jesus' "follow me" to be a call to surrender to Jesus' lordship, to make him the focus of our devotion, and to become more and more like him in how we think and speak and live. When we begin the journey of following Jesus in this way, we become his disciples; we begin the journey of 'discipleship.' Bible scholar Willard Swartley points out that

> John expresses "believe *in* Jesus" using the Greek preposition *eis*, which literally means *into*. It denotes "movement toward." Hence belief in Jesus leads to orienting one's life in the direction of Jesus, moving closer and closer to him. To refuse belief means the opposite: moving further away from Jesus." (Swartley 2013, 505)

Discipleship is the Essence of the Christian Faith

One of the primary emphases of the early Anabaptists was that true conversion, a true surrender to Christ, will necessarily become obvious in how we behave. They said that one truly surrendered to Jesus will begin to think and speak and treat people in more God-honoring ways. They were dismayed at how little Christlikeness they saw in people who were supposedly good Christians. They understood from the New Testament that Christians are those who keep the commands of Jesus and his apostles to live loving and holy lives by the regenerating power of the Holy Spirit at work within them.

In *The Anabaptist Vision*, Harold Bender says that Anabaptists consider discipleship to be the essence of the Christian faith. He writes,

> The Anabaptists were concerned most of all about "a true Christian life," that is, a life patterned after the teaching and example of Christ. . . . The Reformation emphasis on faith [especially by Luther and later by Calvin] was good, but inadequate, for without newness of life, they held, faith is hypocritical. . . . The focus of the Christian life was to be not so much the inward experience of the grace of God, as it was for Luther, but the outward application of that grace to all human conduct. (Bender 1944, 16, 20-21)

For Anabaptists, repenting and believing in Jesus was not just a momentary decision about one's future fate. It meant embracing a whole new way of living. It meant beginning the journey of following in the way of Jesus. Especially for Luther, but also for other reformers, the primary good news was that faith in the mercy and power of God provides us with freedom from guilt and the assurance of forgiveness of our sins. For Anabaptists, the good news included those things but was more focused on the way the power of God enables us to live out the commands of Jesus. For them, the even better news was that believers are free to be regenerated, to be made new, by the power of the Holy Spirit at work within us.

It's crucial to keep in mind, as we noted in chapter 4, that Christlikeness isn't something we accomplish on our own. It can only happen by the power of the Holy Spirit at work within us. But we also believe Jesus taught that if the Holy Spirit really is changing us from within, none of us will be able to hide the results. It's incredibly good news that God's saving work in our lives includes a process of transforming us to look, think, and act more and more like Jesus.

That's why Anabaptists contend there's no such thing biblically, in either the Old Testament or New Testament, as a conversion that does not impact how you live. We see the emphasis of the other reformers on "faith alone" as an overreaction to the rituals and ceremonies Luther denounced as human-made barriers that kept people from being reconciled to God.

The problem with a primary emphasis on faith alone is that it tends to reduce a choice to surrender to Jesus to an individual, internal, or intellectual experience rather than considering it the beginning of a whole new way of life as part of a reconciled and reconciling faith community. Even Martin Luther acknowledged as much later in his life; he expressed disappointment and regret that there was so little true life change among his followers (Bender 1944, 17).

We are forgiven and transformed by the Holy Spirit not as an end in itself but so we can obey God, live holy lives together in the world, and see the kingdom of God come to life among us and through us. Discipleship is actually living a different way of life, not just accepting a set of beliefs. Anabaptists understood Jesus to teach that a truly changed life is more important than any formula someone recites to be converted or whatever internal, emotional experience someone might or might not have as part of their conversion. They said you could tell who was sincerely converted by looking at how they lived their lives and at how they treated the people around them.

This emphasis was clear to them throughout the teachings of Jesus but specifically in the Sermon on the Mount and in passages like John 14:15 "If you love me, keep my commandments" and Luke 14:27 "If you do not carry your own cross and follow me, you cannot be my disciple" (NLT).

Thankfully, the call to discipleship, to truly regenerated lives, is much clearer and much more widely shared in evangelical Christian teaching today than it seems to have been in the 1500s. For example, Dallas Willard has helpfully pointed out that discipleship is learning from Jesus how to live my life as Jesus himself would if he were in my place (Willard 1997, 291).

I still remember being caught off guard in a seminar for church leaders by the simple and very appropriate question, "What is your congregation's process for making disciples?" We were busy offering many programs and services, but even though we were a Mennonite congregation, we had not examined them closely with that big picture question in mind. Ministry leaders now have an overwhelming variety of models, books, and curricula available to help us make disciples rather than merely calling people to an inner intellectual conversion.

The Priesthood of All Believers

In his challenge to the Roman Catholic Church, Martin Luther denounced the need for mediators in our relationship with God. He said the New Testament teaches that every individual has direct access to God without the need for go-betweens, that we all have equal standing as children of God. There are no more or less important Christians in the church. We all share in the responsibility of ministering to each other in the community of believers. This teaching came to be known as "the priesthood of all believers," although Luther never used that phrase himself.

Menno Simons agreed with Luther as far as he went on this point, but Simons extended it by framing it in an Anabaptist perspective. Simons said the priesthood of all believers also means believers are all called to the high standard of living that priests are called to. We are all called to live holy lives that bring to life the teachings and example of Jesus and to thereby witness to the reality and truth of the gospel.

This emphasis drew attention to them in a time when Anabaptists were considered heretics and were being persecuted for not complying with the blended power and authority of the church and state. Their emphasis on living holy lives was unusual enough in their time that anyone living a pious Christian life could be suspected of being an Anabaptist heretic.

In his 1582 book, *Against the Terrible Errors of the Anabaptists*, Roman Catholic theologian Franz Agricola acknowledged that their behavior was "irreproachable." He wrote that among the Anabaptists there was "no lying, deception, swearing, strife, . . . [or] intemperate eating and drinking." Instead, they lived in "humility, patience, uprightness, neatness, honesty, temperance, straightforwardness in such measure that one would suppose that they had the Holy Spirit of God."

I understand him to have meant, "If we didn't know better, we might think the Holy Spirit was at work within and among them based on how they live their lives!" On the other hand, in 1562 a German court realized Casper Zacher could not be an Anabaptist because he was envious and quarrelsome, used profanity, and carried a weapon (Bender 1944, 24, 26).

As we noted in chapter 1, although the Anabaptists embraced the content of the Apostles' Creed and Nicene Creed, they thought it was very unfortunate that both completely ignore Jesus' life, teachings, and larger mission of calling together a regenerated people who would follow him in everyday life (Hershberger 2013, 161).

Earning Your Salvation

One of the most frequent criticisms of the Anabaptist emphasis on discipleship from other Christians is that it places too much weight on our response to God. These critics think Anabaptists are actually teaching that we earn our salvation (our reconciliation with God) with our right behavior.

Of course, that's not the way Anabaptists understand it, but the critics have a valid point. When we have lost touch with Paul's teaching in 1 Corinthians 13 on the importance of grounding all of what we do in love, a determined focus on people's behavior (on how well they are following) has sometimes hardened into legalism among Anabaptists. When we pay more attention to how someone is dressed or to their means of transportation or to their media habits than we do to their character and maturity, we have erred on the "earning" side of this tension.

On the other hand, in the great commission, Jesus commands his followers to make disciples, not just to win converts. The proper understanding of what it means to make disciples is that a sincere inner surrender to Jesus often comes first but our surrender then becomes obvious as we live truly surrendered lives as described and lived by Jesus, because the Holy Spirit's transformative power simply cannot be hidden. It will inevitably leak out in some combination of more love, more joy, more peace, more patience, more kindness, more goodness, greater faithfulness, more gentleness, greater self-control, and so on.

Of course, our behaviors also affect our inner realities. In the flow of our lives, our beliefs shape our practices and our practices shape or deepen our beliefs. This cycle forms both our thinking and living, so our behaviors and our beliefs are both critically important in our walk with Jesus.

If you read John 15 carefully (remain in me and I will remain in you), you realize that in this passage Jesus completely intertwines what God does and what we do. God acts, but we act, too. God prunes, purifies, remains in, loves, chooses, and appoints us. We remain in him, produce fruit, go, love each other, do what he commands, and bring glory to God. Without him, we can do nothing, but in him, we are expected to do amazing things. God gives us the ability to follow, but we have to use that ability and actually follow. Reconciliation comes first. Changed lives follow. We don't try to change our lives because we hope that God will then be willing to be reconciled with us. In other words, following Jesus is something we do in the power and by the grace of God not to earn our salvation but because we live in the freedom and joy of the beloved children of God.

Eyam, 1665

One of my favorite stories of discipleship in action, showing the interplay of God's transforming power and human action, comes from the tiny English village of Eyam. I found this story, told in many online sources with sometimes varying details, during Covid season and have been inspired by it ever since.

In 1665, the bubonic plague flared up again in Eyam in north central England. At that time, Eyam was a village of no more than 800 people—estimates range from 400 to 800. The plague first claimed the life of the tailor but quickly spread to his family and neighbors. The first impulse of most people was to leave town to get away from the disease. The problem was that they had no way to know who was already infected in Eyam, but they knew the infection had not yet spread to other local villages. If they all fled Eyam for the safety of the surrounding villages, they might launch a new wave of the disease that would impact their whole region.

The town's Anglican minister persuaded the people of Eyam to stay put and not to flee. They realized they could prevent the plague from spreading to other towns and villages by staying, even though they all knew many of them would die. The people of Eyam agreed to serve their neighbors in the surrounding villages by quarantining themselves until the disease had passed. They put a ring of stones around the village so everyone could see a physical line they should not cross. People from neighboring villages who understood what was happening gratefully left food and other supplies by the stones, so no one would have to cross the line of stones in either direction.

The people of Eyam held their worship services outside with families standing at a distance from each other—they were social distancing in 1665. It took a full year for the plague to spend itself in Eyam. The suffering was terrible. More than 250 people died, including the wife of the Anglican minister. One woman, Elizabeth Hancock, buried her husband and all six of her children who all died within eight days of each other. Whole families were wiped out. About half of the villagers died that year. But the brave and courageous people of Eyam stood together and prevented the spread of the plague to the people around them.

What an incredible true story of the love and power of God in action. As you think about the interplay between the power of God and the actions of the people in this story, also consider the dynamics in the stories from the Bible, and think about how you would answer the following questions.

- Did God *make* the people of Eyam do this? Did God make their decisions for them? Should we conclude that this was entirely a direct act of God?
- Did the people of Eyam do this entirely in their own strength? Did they decide to risk their lives and withstand the death of so many of their loved ones without any capacity beyond their own?

My answer to all of these questions is "No, I don't think so!" I would say it's a much better fit to Jesus' teaching in John 15 and to my experience of making difficult decisions to conclude that the people of Eyam followed the example and commandment of Jesus (to love each other in the same way I have loved you, John 15:12). I believe they loved in the power and by the grace of God at work within them and among them.

In his love for us, Jesus gave up his life for us on the cross. The people of Eyam did the same thing when faced with the plague. In December 2024, former rector of Eyam Parish Church Mike Gilbert told me, "It was definitely the hope of heaven that kept them going in the face of incredible fear, unimaginable uncertainty, and a mounting death toll."

Nonconformity

Several years ago, I got a phone call from an acquaintance I'll call "Doug." Doug was someone about my age I had thought might become a friend, so when he invited me and my wife over for dessert to get to know us better, we happily accepted.

At some point, our conversation shifted dramatically when he looked at me and said, "Karl, what are your goals for your life?" I stammered a little, not realizing we would get to life goals so soon, but I didn't really mind answering the question. I told Doug I wanted to enjoy a thriving, lifelong marriage with my wife; I wanted to be a man of integrity and outstanding character; and since I was in graduate school at the time, I wanted to complete my training program and earn my degree at the university.

Doug looked a little puzzled, as if those had never occurred to him as possible answers to his question. He responded, "Okay, but what about things like vacations, boats, or a nice house? What are your *financial* goals?"

It was my turn to be puzzled. I recognized those as things I would be happy to enjoy, but I didn't really think of them as goals for my life. As the conversation unfolded from there, it became clear that he was hoping I would sign up for what he called "a business opportunity," a business arrangement that could help me but also benefit him financially. After I declined, he seemed less interested in getting to know us better.

Over the next few weeks, as I sifted through my thoughts and feelings about what happened in our evening with Doug, I decided I didn't really mind that he saw me as a prospect for his business opportunity. I realized that he was just trying to provide for his family, and I was trying to do the same thing.

What bothered me was that he didn't tell me that up front. He didn't say, "Hey Karl, please come over to my house so I can tell you about a business opportunity I'm really excited about and that I think would be perfect for you." What I minded was that his approach felt less than straightforward. I was also a little hurt and disappointed that his interest in me seemed to have more to do with the money he could make from me rather than deepening a brotherly connection. He traded in a bit of my trust in the people of our congregation in the hopes of making some money.

That experience came back to mind for me recently when studying the story in Matthew 20:17-28. There two of Jesus' closest followers, James and John, had their mother ask Jesus to promise them seats of privilege and power in his kingdom. Matthew doesn't tell us what they had in mind when asking for this favor, but it seems reasonable to assume that they were asking for power and authority and maybe hoping for privilege, status, and wealth. I imagine they wanted to be successful and to be seen as successful by the people around them. That probably sounds rather familiar. Most of us would also like to be successful and to be seen as successful by the people around us.

But of course, Jesus responds to their request by saying, That's not how it works in my kingdom. Power, privilege, status, and wealth are not the goals in my kingdom. In my kingdom, the focus is loving service. The people who are considered great in my kingdom are the ones who serve the most completely and the most faithfully. Or rephrasing this using the language of chapter 3 (We are citizens of two kingdoms), we might say, "As my followers you will be living in the kingdom of the world, but you will be living by the standards of the kingdom of God."

Paul says something similar in Romans 12:2: "Do not be conformed to this world, but be transformed by the renewing of your minds, so that you may discern what is the will of God— what is good and acceptable and perfect" (NRSV). In other words, do not live by (do not conform to) the standards of people around you who are not following Jesus. People who are not surrendered to the lordship of Jesus are going to be living by different standards than you are. In fact, the way we live in the kingdom of God will sometimes look completely upside-down to people living by the standards of the kingdom of the world (Kraybill 2003).

I continue to be inspired by the stories of Mennonites I know who have chosen nonconformity in their embrace of simplicity and their disregard for conventional standards of success. One is a medical doctor with a very high income who lives well below his means to generously support kingdom causes. Another is a farmer who maintained his commitment to give away thirty percent of his income even in the year he had to borrow money to buy groceries. He did so again in the year when insurance didn't cover all the damage caused by an electrical storm.

Another is an engineer who resolved to give a tithe of his working years in addition to a tithe of his income. He estimated that he would work for thirty years, which meant a ten percent tithe of three years. He was so engaged with the mission work he did during those three years that he extended them to ten. When he retired, he remembered those first ten years fondly as "one of the most fulfilling times of my life."

If discipleship is the positive side of following Jesus, for Anabaptists, as Harold Bender puts it, nonconformity is the negative side. Discipleship is what we *do*. Conforming to the world is what we do *not* do (Bender 1944, 28). This is the practical outworking of the reality that, between Jesus' first coming and his second coming, we live in two distinctly different kingdoms.

Our goal is to conform to the kingdom of God rather than to conform to the kingdom of the world in how we think, speak, and conduct ourselves. Unfortunately, for Anabaptist groups, nonconformity has sometimes degenerated into being far less clear and specific about what followers of Jesus *will* do than it is about what we *will not* do.

Anabaptist groups vary in terms of how they define nonconformity. When people ask how Mennonites are different from the Amish, I usually tell them we are theological cousins. We all agree that the lives of people following Jesus should be noticeably different from the lives of people who are not following Jesus. The main difference is in how we define nonconformity, that is, in *how* our lives should be different.

Amish and other more "conservative" Anabaptist groups each have a unique and detailed list of lifestyle matters that specify how members of each group will decline to conform to the world around them in a shared way. For example, the Amish groups near where I live dress alike in solid colors, adopt common hairstyles, prohibit the use of bicycles, drive gray buggies, and don't connect to the electrical grid. Hutterites include communal living as part of their nonconformity.

From 1881 until 1981 when it was rescinded (it was revised multiple times), Lancaster Mennonite Conference (LMC) Mennonites were expected to live within the guidelines of a printed "Rules and Discipline" booklet. Less "conservative" Anabaptist groups, including LMC Mennonites, now generally let individuals or congregations make their own decisions about how to live differently from the people around them who are not following Jesus. But the underlying principle of nonconformity for Jesus followers is a shared theme in all of these groups.

Whole-Life Discipleship

We are now able to connect the dots between two core beliefs in the Anabaptist framework. If Jesus really is Lord of absolutely everything (core belief #1) and if following him (discipleship) means living by his standards (core belief #4), then it follows that his standards apply to absolutely every part of our lives. This means that everything about who I am, every hope or dream I have, everything I own, needs to be surrendered to Jesus. There's no distinction in the teachings of Jesus and his apostles between our public lives and our private lives. We are called to follow Jesus faithfully in any and all parts of our lives and in any and all circumstances. Jesus calls me, he calls us, to whole-life discipleship (Bender 1944, 20).

Whole-life discipleship means there's nothing in my life that does not fall under the Lordship of Jesus. Nothing I have is really mine—not my mind, my body, my health, my emotions, or my behavior, not my abilities, my time, my power, my work, my opportunities, my advantages, my money or my stuff, not my marriage, my family, or my relationships.

None of those things ultimately belong to me once I surrender to the Lordship of Jesus and begin to align myself with that reality. All of these things need to be handled and treated in ways that conform to his standards and not in ways that conform to the standards of the world. All of these things have been entrusted to me by the one who truly owns them for me to enjoy, to care for, and to use to serve other people.

Whole-life discipleship is also grounded in our understanding of creation. Psalm 24:1-2 reads, "The earth is the Lord's, and everything in it, the world, and all who live in it; for he founded it on the seas and established it on the waters." If God created everything and all who live in the world, then he owns all of it and all of us.

For the Mennonites who settled in Lancaster County, Pennsylvania, in the early 1700s, these verses were a central focus. They understood that, if the whole earth was created by God, then even the land they had come to own and had been owned by others before them (see Ruth 2021), ultimately belongs to God. They saw this as a mandate to care for the earth as a gift from God. The book that tells their story is titled *The Earth Is the Lord's* (Ruth 2001).

Summary

We become part of the kingdom of God when we choose to follow Jesus. The truth is that every human being is following someone or something external to themselves. Everyone is living up to standards that have come to them from a social group whether they realize it or not. Christians have embraced this reality and have consciously chosen to follow Jesus in everyday life and to live up to his standards.

Surrendering your life to Jesus, surrendering to his lordship and to following him means far more than just appreciating him or agreeing with him in some general way. It's much more than being intellectually persuaded by his teaching or impressed by his example. It even means much more than just praying a brief "sinner's prayer."

Anabaptists believe Jesus called us to live our lives differently than we would if we were not following him. We *follow* Jesus in everyday life. That means we seek to live out his call and to live up to his standards rather than living by the standards of the world around us. The stories of James and John and my friend Doug are examples of the many ways our dreams and our behavior can be more conformed to the standards of the world than to the standards of the kingdom of God.

The lives of those who have truly surrendered their lives to the lordship of Jesus will be noticeably different from what they would be if they were following someone else or seeking to live by some other standard.

NOTE: You can read more about the themes covered in this chapter in the following articles of the Confession of Faith in a Mennonite Perspective—3: Holy Spirit, 10: The church in mission, 15: Ministry and Leadership, 17: Discipleship and the Christian life, and 18: Christian spirituality.

Chapter 6

We Follow Jesus Together

Core belief 5: Together

My wife and I flew from Baltimore, Maryland, to Denver, Colorado, in December 2022 to celebrate Christmas with our children and grandchildren. We were two of the many thousands of people stranded by Southwest Airlines over the holidays that year. Our flight to Chicago was uneventful, but after a long delay our connecting flight to Denver was canceled along with many other flights. We spent two nights in a hotel near O'Hare Airport before renting a car and driving fifteen hours to finish our trip to Denver.

Thankfully, we had planned to be away more than a few days, so we still got to enjoy lazy days, two snowfalls, many meals, long talks, several football games, board games, and walks together with our children, their spouses, and our granddaughters. We enjoyed a rich and memorable time of being together, catching up with each other, and generating new family memories.

One of the days we were in Colorado was January 1, which happened to be the day my parents, brother and sister-in-law, nieces, nephews, and grand-nephews got together. So on January 1, even though we were with one part of our family, we missed gathering with another part of our family. As it happened, January 1, 2023, was also a Sunday, so our congregation back home in Pennsylvania gathered for worship that day. By being with part of our natural family, we missed a day of worship and teaching and fellowship with our brothers and sisters in Christ. We missed a gathering of our spiritual family.

As Followers of Jesus, We Are Part of a New Type of Family

As discussed in chapter 3, one of the deep and wonderful truths of becoming a follower of Jesus is that when we confess our sins and surrender our lives to him, we are reconciled with God. Our sins are forgiven, the power of sin is broken in our lives, and the Holy Spirit comes to live within us to make possible a whole new way of living. That is terrifically good news.

A second deep and wonderful truth of becoming a follower of Jesus (there are many more!) is that we become part of the family of people (the community) who are following Jesus like we are. We are joined with the people of God here in our town, in our county, in our state, and all over the world as God reshapes the way we treat each other and works through us to change the world. My conversion to becoming a follower of Jesus is as much about joining the people of God as it is about being saved from my sin.

We saw in chapter 3 that God's mission in the world is to reconcile all things to himself through Jesus Christ. We reviewed the four relationships that have been broken by sin and which God is now repairing through the person and work of Jesus. God's full shalom will include the full restoration of all four relationships. The second core belief discussed in chapter 3 is that "The kingdom of God is where people unite under the lordship of Jesus."

Here in chapter 6, our focus is on the restoration of the second broken relationship—our reconciliation with each other. Anabaptists believe Jesus taught that our reconciliation with God necessarily leads to us being reconciled with each other and that God intends to accomplish things through us as a community that could never be accomplished through individuals acting alone. The fifth core belief is that "We follow Jesus *together*." We believe that being an active and involved part of a local Christian faith community (usually a church or congregation) is an indispensable component of following Jesus.

As we live in obedience to Jesus' main command to his disciples in John 15:12 to "Love one another as I have loved you," Paul says that God will be building us together into a dwelling in which God lives by his spirit. It's true that God the Holy Spirit lives within each individual Christian, but it's also important to realize that the Holy Spirit also uniquely indwells the gathered community of God's people. We are "being built *together*" into a dwelling place for God.

> In Christ Jesus you who once were far away have been brought near by the blood of Christ. For he himself is our peace, who has made the two groups one and has destroyed the barrier, the dividing wall of hostility, by setting aside in his flesh the law with its commands and regulations. **His purpose was to create in himself one new humanity out of the two, thus making peace**, and in one body to reconcile both of them to God through the cross, by which **he put to death their hostility**. He came and preached peace to you who were far away and peace to those who were near.
>
> For through him we both have access to the Father by one Spirit. Consequently, you are no longer foreigners and strangers, but fellow citizens with God's people and also members of his household, built on the foundation of the apostles and prophets, with Christ Jesus himself as the chief cornerstone. In him the whole building is joined together and rises to become a holy temple in the Lord. And in him **you too are being built together to become a dwelling in which God lives by his Spirit**. (Eph. 2:13-22)

In Christ Jesus, God has destroyed the hostility that once divided us from each other because of our earthly differences. His purpose has always been to re-create one new humanity by reconciling all of us to him and to each other through the cross. No one who is surrendered to following Jesus is considered an outsider anymore. We are all now at peace with each other. All of us are being joined together as a holy, living temple in which God is present and is seen to be present. When you look at our gathered faith communities, you should be able to see the living, active presence of God the Holy Spirit blazing away and bursting out.

So following Jesus is a choice we make freely, for ourselves (chapter 4), but implications of that choice reach far beyond just me and my own life. We see a picture of this when two people marry. When you marry someone, you choose to commit to them, to join your lives in a deep and rich way. But, if you didn't already know this, you quickly discover that your new husband or new wife is still part of a larger family! You realize that you have not only joined your life to another person. By choosing to marry, you have chosen to become part of a whole new family that may be very different from the one you have known so far.

Even if you or your spouse are not in close touch with that new family, you also quickly learn that your new wife's or new husband's habits have been deeply shaped by that other family—everything from how you load toilet paper rolls, what goes in the refrigerator and what doesn't, how you do or do not express anger, how you resolve conflicts, and how you celebrate holidays, to name just a few.

The same is true when you become a follower of Jesus. You join a whole new family! And it may be very different from the one you have known so far.

There are two crucial things to know about this new family you have joined. First, none of us in this new family belong to ourselves anymore. Each of us and all of us now belong to God. As we saw in Chapter 5, whole life discipleship means that our lives, our priorities, our work, our bodies, our money, our time, our stuff, even our natural families all belong to God. God now sets the standard for how we handle all of those things.

The apostle Paul wrote,

> Do you not know that your bodies are temples of the Holy Spirit, who is in you, whom you have received from God? **You are not your own**; you were bought at a price. Therefore honor God with your bodies. (1 Cor. 6:19-20)

My paraphrase of what Paul is saying is "You don't own yourself." The context in 1 Corinthians is sexual behavior, but the principle applies broadly. Following Jesus changes everything about how we think about the future, set priorities, care for our bodies, manage our money, manage our time, relate to our spouses and our families, and care for people in need. One of the important things we do together in Christian community is help each other figure out how to honor God in all these different parts of our lives. For example, what does it mean for me to surrender my car to God? To surrender my money? To surrender my time? And so on.

Second, the main way we show our love for God in this new family is by loving each other. The author of the letter we know as 1 John puts this very bluntly:

> We love each other because he loved us first. If someone says, "I love God," but hates a fellow believer, that person is a liar; **for if we don't love people we can see, how can we love God, whom we cannot see**? And he has given us this command: **Those who love God must also love their fellow believers**. (1 John 4:19-21, NLT)

One of the main things we do as followers of Jesus is love each other well. In the community of Jesus followers (in this new family), people we would not expect to love and serve each other in the outside world do so within the family of Jesus. Rich people and poor people love and serve each other. Young people and old people love and serve each other. White, black, Hispanic, Asian people love and serve each other. And in the U.S., even Republicans and Democrats and Libertarians love and serve each other.

Wherever we see all this happening in our world, we see a foretaste of the new creation, a sample of the way things will be when all things are restored. If we are part of this community, we get a foretaste of heaven itself, of God's full shalom. But of course, this isn't how most people live their lives. And it's not the life that's glorified in our television shows, in our movies, in popular culture, on social media, in our politics, and maybe not even in our conversations or in the lives of the people around us. But it's the life that God calls us to live if we are followers of Jesus.

Church as Community

In *The Anabaptist Vision*, Harold Bender identifies three distinctive elements of that vision. We discussed the first of these in chapter 5—discipleship is the essence of the Christian faith. The second is a new concept of the church as "**a brotherhood of love** in which the fullness of the Christian life ideal is to be expressed.... Basic to the Anabaptist vision of the church was the insistence on **the practice of true brotherhood and love among the members of the church**" (Bender 1944, 29, 34). In today's language, we would say a "community of love" and insist on the practice of "true community" and love among the members of the church.

Bender goes on to say that this is not understood as merely a pious sentiment but as a commitment to meet each other's needs by actually sharing our possessions with each other. This practice came to be known as "mutual aid."

Bender also said that "the absolutely essential heart" of this new concept of the church, based on the teachings of Jesus and his apostles, is "voluntary church membership based upon true conversion and involving a commitment to holy living and discipleship" (Bender 1944, 26). We engaged these two parts in chapter 4 on choosing and chapter 5 on following/discipleship. Core belief #5 on Christian community (following *together*) is grounded in those core beliefs.

So, for Anabaptists, "church" or "going to church" isn't simply an individual activity I might do when I feel like it or when I need something from it. It isn't simply a weekly chore I complete to placate God. For us, being part of a "church" means sharing together in the rich life of the kingdom of God that's unfolding among a particular group of Jesus followers.

Just as our following of Jesus is a whole life commitment, so too our participation in our local faith community (usually a congregation) is a wide-ranging commitment to the well-being and flourishing of our brothers and sisters in this new family and of the community as a whole. Just as we sometimes limit other commitments to make time for our natural family, we also limit other commitments so we can invest time and energy into the life of our local Christian community.

As individualists, we Americans tend to read the New Testament as though it were written primarily to individuals. We tend to assume all the instructions and other verbs are singular when in fact most of them are plural. Many Americans seem to believe that the main point of Jesus' teachings and work was to secure heaven for individuals. A more faithful reading, however, recognizes that the main point of Jesus' mission was to form a new community, what Ron Sider calls "a reconciled and reconciling community" (Sider 1999, 76).

The New Testament is full of instructions on how to treat each other within the Christian community. For example, if you search for the phrase "one another," you will find almost fifty such instructions, including love one another, honor one another, forgive one another, encourage one another, greet one another, and live in harmony with one another. You can't obey any of these instructions all on your own. You have to be part of a Christian faith community to do these things.

We believe Jesus and his apostles intended "church" to be a community of love in which the fullness of the Christian life ideal is expressed and where we live out true community and truly love and serve each other as members of this community. As Scot McKnight puts it, from start to finish throughout the story the Bible tells

> the work of God is *to form a community* in which the will of God is done and through which one finds both union with God and communion with others for the good of others and the world. (McKnight 2007, 119, emphasis in the original)

One of the tensions this raises is that the focus and energy of a faith community naturally drifts inward over time. Members gradually spend more and more time and energy on relationships and activities within the community rather than those outside the community. But as we saw chapter 3, God also invites us to join him in extending reconciliation and peace beyond the Christian community, out into the world around us. Yes, the assurance of true reconciliation with God and true reconciliation with each other is incredibly good news. But in the drama of God's work in the world, those two developments are just the first steps of God's even larger project of reconciling the entire world to himself in Christ. The reconciled and reconciling community of God's people is also meant to be the launch pad for our shared ministry of reconciliation to people outside our faith communities.

On the other hand, I object when I hear people say that the church is the one organization that exists for the benefit of non-members. People who say that often do so because they are frustrated with a congregation's lack of outward focus. That frustration is valid, but the full truth is that the church exists for the sake of both its members and its non-members. It's astonishing and wonderful that in Jesus so many different kinds of people are being drawn together into the joy of life in a loving community in which God lives by his spirit. But we should also never lose sight of our shared mission to be a holy and priestly community to the world and for the sake of the world around us.

Mutual Aid

As members of a healthy Christian community, we seek to meet each other's needs just like the earliest Christians did in Acts 2 when they even sold property and possessions to help brothers and sisters who were in need. John even urges us to go to the extent of "lay[ing] down our lives" for each other.

> This is how we know what love is: Jesus Christ laid down his life for us. And we ought to **lay down our lives for our brothers and sisters.** If anyone has material possessions and sees a brother or sister in need but has no pity on them, how can the love of God be in that person? (1 John 3:16-17)

The Anabaptist emphasis on mutual aid, on meeting each other's needs within the Christian community, is grounded in the emphasis presented in chapter 3 on the distinction between the kingdom of God and the kingdom of the world. In part because of how the power of the state was used to carry out the wishes of the Anabaptists' opponents in the church to persecute, imprison, and kill them in the 1500s, they strongly advocated a complete separation between the church and the state.

That extended to refusing to rely on the state or other secular groups for any kind of support. They believed that Christians should meet each other's needs and provide for anyone in need within the Christian community. They saw this as part of truly loving and serving each other and as an important way to live out our willingness to lay down our lives for each other in obedience to Jesus' command to 'love each other as I have loved you.'

Over the centuries, Anabaptists have worked together within their faith communities to provide interest free loans to each other and to respond to fire and storm damage to their properties. Many resisted participation in secular insurance companies, believing that Christians should meet each other's needs rather than turning to outside sources to help manage risk. Other types of mutual aid have included burial aid societies, hospital and medical aid societies, automobile accident insurance plans, and retirement savings plans.

One of the unintended consequences of this approach has sometimes been that the larger and more visible these mutual aid groups become, the more they look like an exclusive club to anyone who might want to participate but is not eligible. Also, when Anabaptist groups have formed large, tight-knit communities that have begun to include business connections, especially when those ties have been consolidated across multiple generations, people outside these communities can feel excluded.

When the insiders of such communities are joined by a shared faith commitment, it's easy to understand why people on the outside might feel excluded by the faith itself, not just by the business ties. When that happens, it means we have let "taking care of each other" get in the way of our mission to be a holy and priestly community that draws in a growing number of people from the world around us.

Yieldedness

The early Anabaptists understood their surrender to the lordship of Jesus to include letting go of self-concern. They sought to be fully yielded to the will of God. The German word they used to express this idea, *Gelassenheit*, doesn't translate very well into English. It means yieldedness (to God's will), letting go, or self-abandonment. It was one of the main convictions that enabled them to endure torture and martyrdom. They believed that it was God's will for them to endure suffering (for them, the baptism of blood) as Jesus did, and the proper response was a stance of yieldedness.

We will have more to say about this in chapter 7, but the connection here is that this basic understanding shifted over time into an expectation that believers would yield to the direction of their faith communities. In other words, many Anabaptists came to see one's willingness to yield to the direction of the group (the church) as the clearest measure of one's willingness to yield to God. You were expected to live out your decision to surrender to Jesus by following and surrendering to the direction of the group (the church), especially in regard to its definition of nonconformity.

Unfortunately, too often this degenerated into an overemphasis on compliant behavior (including at times, for example, wearing a prayer veiling for women, a plain suit for men, not owning a radio or TV) if you wanted to be a member in good standing. For many people, this eventually became a journey through a joyless legalism, in which following Jesus was defined more by keeping the rules than by growing in love, character, and Christlikeness. For that reason, some Anabaptist groups eventually rescinded their "Rules and Discipline" guidelines.

On the other hand, a proper experience of yielding to the group (yielding to the church) as part of our yieldedness to God is an important part of following Jesus *together*. All of the "one another-ing" passages mentioned above call us to deference, humility, and forbearance in our life together in the Christian community. Paul urges us not to be overly focused on our own interests but instead and in humility to look out for the interests of others (Phil. 2:3-4).

Our call is to lovingly serve the well-being and flourishing of our brothers and sisters even when that may sometimes mean setting aside our own interests. We continue to highly value and to grow in our ability to cooperate graciously and lovingly in Christian community.

The tension between sacrificially yielding to the community and standing up for yourself is a good example of "a tension to manage" rather than "a problem to solve," especially for those of us who are so deeply formed by individualism and consumerism (see below). Obviously, we have a responsibility to care for ourselves and our families, but we also have a responsibility to care for one another in the Christian community, even when it costs us. After all, our call is to "lay down our lives for each other" as brothers and sisters in the family of God.

When these two responsibilities conflict with each other, we seek to make wise decisions about where to spend our time, energy, and resources. Our larger goal will continue to be that everyone is well cared for and flourishing, so these are priorities for us to balance rather than competing priorities to resolve by choosing one over the other.

Linking Baptism with Church Membership

This core belief—we follow Jesus *together*—is the main reason why Mennonite churches have historically declined to baptize someone who doesn't also commit to active membership in the local body (a stance being debated today). For Anabaptists, participation in the kingdom of God is personal but never private. It certainly includes the individual's reconciliation with God, but that necessarily also includes living out our reconciliation with each other in the family of God as described above in Ephesians 2.

We see this clearly in several places in the New Testament. First, as part of Paul's discussion of how the body of Christ should be a harmonious interworking of component parts in 1 Corinthians 12-14, he writes,

> The human body has many parts, but the many parts make up one whole body. So it is with the body of Christ. Some of us are Jews, some are Gentiles, some are slaves, and some are free. But **we have all been baptized into one body** by one Spirit, and we all share the same Spirit. (1 Cor. 12:12-13, NLT)

In other words, in or through our baptism, we are incorporated into a local body of Christian believers that will be working together harmoniously as we each contribute our gifts to the group to further the mission of the kingdom of God in our part of the world. Later on in verse 27, Paul says each one of us is part of this body, and the whole point of chapter 12 is that none of us can say we don't need each other.

The second place we see this linkage is in Acts 2, which describes the response to Peter's sermon on the day of Pentecost. If we follow the flow of events, we learn in verse 41 that about 3,000 people obeyed Peter's instruction to be baptized. The following verses describe what they did after they were baptized, or, we might say, how the rhythms of their lives were changed by having been baptized.

> **They devoted themselves** to the apostles' teaching and **to fellowship, to the breaking of bread and to prayer**. Everyone was filled with awe at the many wonders and signs performed by the apostles. **All the believers were together and had everything in common.** They sold property and possessions to give to anyone who had need. Every day they **continued to meet together** in the temple courts. **They broke bread in their homes and ate together** with glad and sincere hearts, praising God and enjoying the favor of all the people. (Acts 2:42-47)

They clearly didn't simply head off into their individual lives and focus only on their personal reconciliation with God. No, they joined in the active life of the local community of believers, eating together, praying together, and caring for each other. They joined the flow of life of the growing community of people who were following Jesus together in that place and at that time. Their regular celebration of table fellowship, including the Lord's Supper, reminded them frequently of the basis of their life together: that they were all baptized into one body by one spirit.

Anabaptist theology has always held that true inner conversion will be evident through changes in outer behavior. We see being an active part of a local body of believers as an essential outer expression of true inner conversion.

Holding a Treasure for the Broader Church

The Anabaptist emphasis on the importance of Christian community as an expression of the kingdom of God in the world, on following Jesus *together*, is a treasure we carry for and offer to the broader church. With some important exceptions, most American evangelicals understand salvation in primarily individual terms. Their focus is on conversion and forgiveness for the individual's sins. Participation in a congregation is then often discussed in terms of how that participation benefits the individual's spiritual growth or how it provides a context in which an individual can serve others both inside and outside the congregation.

All of that's fine as far as it goes, but it generally ignores or undervalues the importance of living out the kingdom of God together as the visible expression of the kingdom of God in a local setting. For example, in a mostly very helpful article in *Christianity Today*, Tim Stafford addresses the question "The Church—Why Bother?" (Stafford 2005). This attention-grabbing title expresses the sentiment of the growing number of people who are "self-proclaimed born-again Christians" who say that their spiritual lives have nothing to do with church. That is, they aren't engaged in the life of a congregation.

In the article, Stafford reviews several reasons why they have come to believe "their salvation is between them and God" and why they see the church as only one among many optional resources to help them on their spiritual journey. He acknowledges that helpful resources such as the Bible, biblical teaching, fellowship with other believers, and worship experiences are widely available outside the church.

Even so, Stafford offers three answers to the question of "what's missing?" for Christians who are not connected to a congregation. He offers them as reasons for why they should get connected to a congregation. First, he writes, "you need a church to get baptized and to receive communion." Second, you "need the regular rhythm of public worship." Most importantly you need to experience being physically present with other believers. Finally, you can't fully experience Christ if you are not connected to his body. This third answer isn't very fully explained, but Stafford does say you need to be in an ongoing, serving relationship to and with other believers.

What's interesting about Stafford's approach (which is shared by many American evangelicals) is that it focuses entirely on the experience of the individual and completely ignores the larger "kingdom of God" or "faith community" picture presented here in this chapter and in chapter 3. The words *kingdom, reconciliation,* and *community* don't show up anywhere in the article.

Stafford was writing to people whose understanding of what it means to follow Jesus had been deeply formed by individualism and consumerism without clearly challenging either one. His article might have been strengthened considerably if it had drawn attention to the first sentence of *The Purpose Driven Life*, which is "It's not about you" (Warren 2002, 17).

The broader and more important answer to the "church—why bother?" question from a New Testament perspective is that, in surrendering to Jesus, we take our place in carrying out the mission of God in the world to reconcile all things to himself in Jesus Christ. Our call is to offer ourselves, our abilities, and our resources to the reconciled and reconciling community where the shalom of God is coming to life. Our call is to be an active part of helping the kingdom of God to be seen in action. It includes but is about far more than my individual holiness and peace. It's impossible to "love each other as I have loved you" in the sense intended by Jesus if you are not meaningfully connected to a faith community.

Stafford's three answers are fine as far as they go, but they seem to me to pale in relation to the New Testament's perspective on the church! The gifts and joys and challenges that come to us as followers of Jesus do so in large part through our active and sustained participation in a particular faith community. We're formed into Christlikeness as we love and serve each other and as we join together in the mission of God in the world. None of that is available to those of us who remain disconnected from a faith community, no matter how contented we may feel.

It's Not Easy to Live This Way!

No matter which country you live in, no matter which century you live in, no matter which culture you are from, the way of Jesus is always different in important ways from the way people live their lives without Jesus. It's always countercultural. Here are three important reasons it's hard for us to live this way right now—in our country, in our century, in Western culture.

1. ***Individualism.*** You and I are individualists. Almost everything around us in the United States forms us in individualism.

As an individualist, I am the focus of my world, not my family, not my friends, not my country, not even God. The focus of my thoughts and my priorities is what I want, how I feel, my emotions, what makes me happy, what I think I deserve, how I'm doing. I expect everyone around me to fit into *my* world.

There are some good things about individualism. In cultures that are mainly focused on the family or the clan, individuals can be overlooked or mistreated. It's good to be aware of ourselves—our tastes, our desires, our feelings, our strengths and weaknesses—and how other people treat us. After all Psalm 37:4 really does say, "Take delight in the Lord, and he will give you the desires of your heart."

But individualism makes it harder to love each other well in the family of God, because for an individualist, *my* following of Jesus (my prayers, my songs of worship, my priorities) tends mostly to be focused on "me and Jesus." I tend to mostly be focused on my personal journey and on how I'm doing in my spiritual life.

Many of our contemporary worship songs reinforce this way of thinking and form us more deeply in individualism. You can see this clearly if you pay attention to how many of your favorite worship songs or the songs you sing in worship over the next few weeks are framed in terms of "I and me" rather than "we and us."

Consider one of the most popular worship songs in 2023—"Goodness of God." It's a lovely and heartfelt expression of gratitude for God's mercy, care, and faithfulness to *me*. It guides worshippers in singing about the goodness of God. It's a fine song as far as it goes, but it is entirely focused on my personal journey with God. It completely ignores God's goodness to us together as the people of God.

"Goodness of God" and similar songs would be strengthened considerably (in a theological sense) by simply adding a verse or two that would guide worshippers in singing about the goodness of God to *us* as a gathered people. That would help counter our cultural bias toward individualism. Thankfully, there are other more recently popular worship songs that do this. For example, "House of the Lord" and "Great Are You, Lord" both use "we" and "our" from start to finish!

The challenge is that very few American Christians have been deeply formed with a sense of being part of a gathered people who experience God's presence and work and guidance collectively. We think little about how God has been merciful and caring and faithful to *us* together, to *us* as a faith community. When we do sing songs that use plural pronouns (we, us, our), most of us think of our congregations as collections of individuals rather than as vibrant faith communities in the sense described above.

My point is that the words we sing in worship both express and shape our thinking about what God is doing in the world. It would be wise for our lyrics to at least balance, if not challenge, individualism for Americans instead of reinforcing it.

Another way that individualism interferes with loving each other well is that *my* experience becomes what is most important. The focus of my thoughts about and my priorities for my life, my relationships, and my commitment to my church is on what I want, how I feel, what I think I deserve, how I'm doing. Other people's experiences and well-being are less important to me.

If we sing a worship song that's not my favorite, I focus on my disappointment and might even complain, instead of realizing that my congregation includes a wide variety of people, so maybe this song is someone else's favorite. After all, someone chose for us to sing this song together.

The problem is how can I love and serve you well when all I really care about is *me*? Why would I ever make any sacrifices for you unless that somehow benefits me? The idea that none of us in this new family belong to ourselves anymore will seem completely backwards and nonsensical to an individualist.

2. **Consumerism.** You and I are consumers. We are shoppers! We are used to having choices.

As consumers, we expect other people to produce products and services and experiences we want, and then we expect to be able to pick and choose the products and services and experiences that please us and reject the ones that don't. As a consumer, it's up to other people to please me or satisfy me with the products and services and experiences I want or think I need. When they don't please me, I make a change.

My focus is not on relationships; it's on getting the products and services and experiences I want, when I want them, and in the way I want them. You and I essentially live with a remote control in our hands. We expect to be able to change channels instantly and as often as we please on anyone and anything in which we lose interest.

I really like being a consumer! There are some great things about it. I have enjoyed thousands of products and services and experiences other people have provided for me. I like having many channels, restaurants, schools, stores, webinars, apps, websites, and podcasts to choose from. Your and my imaginations and expectations have been deeply formed by all the years we have spent making an endless series of consumer choices.

Recently, when looking for a new insulated water bottle to keep my coffee as hot as possible, I discovered that there are more than a dozen brands to choose from, that each brand offers dozens of options, and that even when I pick a specific bottle, it comes in fifteen different colors! It was a little overwhelming. But like an experienced consumer, I pressed on. My next step was to compare prices on my brand, model, and color on multiple websites. I happily expected someone else to provide me with variety, high quality, and low prices.

You may see where this is going. Consumerism makes it harder for us to love each other well in the family of God, because you and I are no longer used to maintaining a commitment to anything or anyone that displeases us. We are used to being able to swap out anything that doesn't please us for a replacement that might. I ended up buying several insulated bottles in my quest to find just the right one, because even though I read the specs and reviews carefully, the first two or three just didn't keep my coffee hot enough.

Unfortunately, without realizing, we have begun to think the same way about relationships and faith communities. So for example, if this church doesn't please me, the one down the road might. If someone in this congregation disappoints or offends me, I'm gone. And just as I would not feel obligated to say goodbye when changing favorite restaurants, I see no need to provide closure if I change churches. I just leave. Some of us treat friendships the same way.

For consumers, church also becomes just another program or service or experience that I may or may not choose to use to meet *my* spiritual needs or wants. I tend to think it's up to other people to provide the programs and spiritual experiences I want from church. I also expect the programs and services the church provides to be excellent even if I have not done anything to help make them excellent. When they don't please me, I make a change.

My focus is not on relationships; it's on me getting the programs and experiences I want, when I want them, and in the way I want them. If I support the church financially, even a little bit, I can begin to think I'm actually paying for the programs and the spiritual experiences, so 1.) nothing more should be required from me, and 2.) it's reasonable for me to expect excellence just like I would when paying for any other product or service. I begin to think of my engagement with my congregation as a consumer transaction rather than as my opportunity to take my place in what God is doing in the world.

The problem for me as a consumer-minded follower of Jesus who has been joined to his family is how can I love and serve you well over the long haul if my focus is on the remote control in my hand? If I'm focused on getting the products and services and experiences I want and in the way I want them rather than on our relationship, how will I ever manage to focus on loving you as I have been loved?

3. *Affluence*—Many of us are affluent. That is, many of us, including me, have more than enough money to take care of ourselves and our families.

If you can comfortably provide food, housing, transportation, education, and medical care for yourself and your family, and especially if you have money left over after covering these basics, you are affluent. Many of us have enough extra money to pay other people to do anything we don't want to do ourselves.

Affluence means I have the freedom to do what I want when I want to do it. I can eat out, I can travel, I can buy goods and services I don't really need. It also means I can avoid situations and people I don't like. It means not having to live too close to other people, not having to depend on other people, and maybe even not having to depend on God, except in emergencies. An affluent person's mindset is often "I earned my money. I worked hard for it, so I get to decide how to use it."

On the one hand, affluence is great! Almost every person in the world hopes for the kind of freedom described here. I'm not the richest person I know, but I'm profoundly grateful to be affluent enough to fly to Colorado to be with my children and grandchildren, to go to an occasional football game, and to pay someone else to trim the long row of huge holly trees in my backyard. I realize that not everyone can afford to do those things.

But affluence makes it hard for you and me to love each other well in the family of God, because our affluence means we don't need to rely on close relationships where we give and receive help and care. We can just buy help and care when we need them.

Affluence reduces my need to depend on God or to depend on you for food, housing, transportation, medical care, or many of the other things I need or want. The more affluent I am, the less I think about God as the source of these things and the less I need to work together with other people in my daily life. Our affluence also means we can and do simply avoid people who are different from us or whom we find tiring or who just rub us the wrong way.

The more affluent I am, the more completely I can plan my schedule around my work, my vacation trips, and my hobbies (like my cabin, my beach house, my boat). My relationships in my congregation or in my neighborhood or with people in need have to fit into the time I have left over. I will show up at church or church events whenever I happen to be in town or when I don't have something more fun to do. After all, if I give to my church at all, I'm paying other people to make 'church' happen.

Let me say clearly, though, in case you are beginning to wonder where this is headed, there's nothing wrong with work, vacations, or hobbies. They are all wonderful gifts, and I'm deeply grateful for the opportunities I have to enjoy each one of them! The problem is the opportunity cost of regularly giving them priority over time spent building deep relationships. Every time you are away from home or your neighborhood or your church or people in need, you miss a chance to invest in relationships (to love and serve) in those places.

The challenge most American followers of Jesus face is that individualism, consumerism, and affluence are all good things. We enjoy their benefits every day. For example, when my wife and I traveled to Colorado for Christmas, we were glad to be individualists. *We* wanted to go. We thought the trip would be good and fun for us and strengthen relationships in our family. We enjoyed the benefits of being consumers, because we got to pick the dates, the airline, and the flights we wanted, and we decided how much money and time to spend on the trip. It took some planning for us to be away from our church on January 1, but we knew we could count on other people to carry the worship service in our absence. We were also grateful to be affluent enough to have the money and the paid vacation time to be away from home for almost two weeks and still be able to pay our bills.

The truth is that these three forces are undermining our investment of time and energy in the richness of our community life in many congregations, including Mennonite and Anabaptist congregations. We retain a core belief in following

Jesus together, but these three forces, along with several others, have reduced the amount of time we spend together and the depth of our commitment to a shared life together.

Summary

Following Jesus *together* (core belief #5) flows directly from the belief that the kingdom of God is where people unite under the lordship of Jesus (core belief #2). Jesus and his apostles clearly saw following him as something we do together, not just as individuals. In our Christian communities, we are meant to be more like an extended family traveling somewhere together rather than like random strangers who happen to be on the same bus.

Even though we may differ from each other in many ways, by the power of the Holy Spirit at work within us and among us, we care deeply for each other and look out for each other. We forgive and forebear with each other, and we hang in there together in tough times. We care as much about how the group is doing as we care about how we are doing ourselves.

An important part of the gospel story is that our reconciliation with God makes possible our reconciliation with each other. In fact, a crucial part of God's mission in the world through Jesus is the formation of a people among whom the life of the kingdom of God becomes real in the world. Our call as individuals is to be reconciled with God so that we can be reconciled with each other and find our place among the people of God in this reconciled and reconciling community. It's in the flourishing of this community, in our loving each other as he loved us, that the love and power of God are made real and visible in the world.

It's not easy to live this way in any time or in any culture. It's particularly challenging for affluent people who are steeped in individualism and consumerism. All three of these forces pull us away from engaging deeply in the Christian community that the work of Jesus makes possible for us and to which he calls us as his followers.

NOTE: You can read more about the themes covered in this chapter in the following articles of the Confession of Faith in a Mennonite Perspective—*9: The church of Jesus Christ, 10: The church in mission, 11: Baptism, 14: Discipline in the church , 16: Church order and unity, 19: Family, singleness, and marriage.*

Chapter 7

We Surrender Our Lives in Love Like Jesus Did

Core belief 6: Surrender Our Lives in Love

Would you donate one of your kidneys to a total stranger? Most of us have two kidneys, but if you are a basically healthy person, you probably don't actually need both of them. But for people who don't have even one healthy kidney, a kidney transplant could save their lives.

Several years ago, as reported on the Atrium Health Daily Dose website in 2022, Steve Sanders learned his kidneys were slowly failing due to a rare disease. His decline was slow but certain. An active father of two young children, Steve knew that lifelong dialysis would dramatically change his life.

No one among his family or friends was a match for him, but eventually word of his situation reached a man named Chris Perez through a post Steve made on social media asking for help. When Chris read about Steve and realized they both had young children, Chris felt a prompting to see what he could do to help. Medical testing found him to be a physical match for a man he had never met!

"It was something about his story as a dad. I was imagining a situation like his in which I would need help," said Chris. "I didn't know him but thought let's give this a try—I would want someone to do this for me." When they connected before the surgery, they discovered they had quite a bit in common and began building a friendship that included both of their families. The surgery was successful and gave Steve a whole new lease on life.

In another case, as reported on the New York-Presbyterian website in 2020, a man named Hendrik Gerrits listened to a podcast story on his train ride home one evening about a woman who became a kidney donor to help a stranger. He learned that there are almost 109,000 people on the national organ transplant list. Roughly 92,000 of them are waiting for a kidney. That means that 85 percent of people needing an organ transplant are in need of a healthy kidney.

The donation from the woman in the story jump-started a transplant chain that saved 28 recipients. "I just remember bawling," recalls Henrik. "I was overwhelmed by the power of the story—and I immediately thought, I could do that. . . . I'm also really lucky to have a wife who doesn't blink at any crazy old thing I want to do!"

Doctors say the donor's remaining kidney grows in size and function to compensate—sort of like working out and becoming more effective at what it does. Kidney donations change the lives of the organ recipients, the organ donors, their families, and countless others. It also often forms an unbreakable bond between people who were once strangers and are now linked for life.

Would you do that? Would you donate one of your healthy kidneys to save the life of a stranger? I wish I could easily say yes, but this one is a struggle for me. Of course I would do it for someone close to me, but it seems like a much bigger deal to do this for a stranger.

What stands out to me in these stories is the donors' willingness to take a chance, to put their own health at risk for someone else's sake, and to step into the unknown. I admire their willingness to sacrifice their self-interest on behalf of a stranger and not to insist on putting themselves first.

That sounds uncomfortably like Jesus to me. It reminds me of what Paul says in his letter to the church in Philippi when he writes,

Don't be selfish; don't try to impress others. Be humble, thinking of others as better than yourselves. Don't look out only for your own interests, but take an interest in others, too. You must have the same attitude that Christ Jesus had.

[Here's what I mean:] Though [Jesus] was God, he did not think of equality with God as something to cling to. Instead, he gave up [he emptied himself of] his divine privileges. He took the humble position of a slave and was born as a human being. When he appeared in human form, he humbled himself in obedience to God and died a criminal's death on a cross. (Phil. 2:3-8, NLT)

The Humility of God

One of the most astonishing things we learn about God when we look at Jesus is that the almighty God, the creator and sustainer of all things is, of all things, humble! "Though [Jesus] was God, he did not think of equality with God as something to cling to." Even though he had every right to, as Lord over absolutely everything, he did not see his power or his privilege as God as things to hold on to. "Instead, he gave up his divine privileges." The Greek word translated "gave up" here literally means he "emptied himself" of those things! Think about that: When was the last time you even thought about letting go of all your power, your money, your property, your possessions, your strengths? What would it take for you to consider doing that?

Paul goes on to say that Jesus took the **humble position** of a slave and was born as a human being. When he appeared in human form, he **humbled himself** in obedience to God and **died a criminal's death** on a cross. The force of the Greek grammar of verse 8 might be better captured in paraphrase as "he humbled himself by walking the path of obedience to God all the way to physical death as a human being, even when that meant dying in the most humiliating and painful way possible at the time—by crucifixion!" (Zerbe 2016).

Whenever I ponder the meaning of these developments, I am stunned all over again to realize how far God was and is willing to go to bring about the reconciliation of the four relationships and the restoration of his creation project to his original intent. The price he has been willing to pay to bring that about is beyond incredible to me.

We have lost much of the force of what death by crucifixion meant in its time. We no longer realize the extent of the horror and humiliation it entailed. Maybe the most comparable way of dying we know today is dying in an electric chair. When you die in an electric chair, you are being executed in a humiliating, shameful, and painful way. It's meant as a statement about how awful your crimes have been, so if you are to be executed by an electric chair, you are imprisoned and seen as a criminal beyond hope of redemption.

When the moment arrives, you are strapped in place and experience the shock and searing pain of a strong electrical current. Your terror and the electrical current will probably trigger a loss of control of your bladder or bowels, and you may not be killed by the first shock of current, in which case it will be repeated. This is not a form of death anyone jokes about, and no one wears electric chair earrings or necklace charm or tattoo to be cool.

When Jesus talked about what he did in becoming human and in yielding to death by crucifixion, he called it "denying myself." In Jesus, we see what theologians call "the humility of God." It's astonishing in the extreme to realize that the one who is Lord of absolutely everything loves us, loves his creation, so deeply that he emptied himself of his power and privilege on our behalf. Not only that, but he even further humbled himself by surrendering to a painful and humiliating physical death. It's quite an understatement to say he humbled himself so that we could be reconciled to God.

So we can clearly see Jesus' loving humility in his birth and in his death, but we can also see his humility in several clear ways by the way he lived.

1. First, **he invited people to follow him rather than demanding or forcing them to follow him**, even when that meant his band of followers was only a small minority of all the people who could have followed him. He gave himself to

them fully and patiently. John 13:1 says he loved them to the end. He let other people who were not yet ready to follow him simply to walk away. There is no story where Jesus chases after anyone to talk them into following him. In his humility, he simply offers and invites, even though he clearly knew who he was and what was at stake in his ministry. Jesus' approach to calling followers is part of the basis for our understanding that people get to *choose* to follow Jesus (core belief #3 presented in chapter 4).

2. A second way ***we see Jesus' humility is in his love for and his patience with his enemies***. Throughout his ministry, he called them to repent, he answered their repeated challenges, and he taught his disciples to follow his example by loving their enemies, too. His approach was to pray for them and to hope for their flourishing in the life of the kingdom of God.

3. A third way ***we see his humility flows from the second, which is that he forgave the people who persecuted him***, those who mistreated him, and those who wronged him. He definitely clashed with them and challenged them, even sharply at times, but who can forget his incredible prayer of loving humility from the cross for his executioners in the face of their mockery, when he said, "Father, forgive them, for they do not know what they are doing" (Luke 23:34).

4. A fourth way ***we see his humility is in his willingness to suffer for the sake of the kingdom of God without retaliation***. He did not plot or scheme against anyone. He made no attempts to destroy his opponents, and he did not even defend himself from them. He simply endured the slander, the taunts, and the challenges. He rejected violence and reprimanded his disciples when they wanted to call down fire on a hostile village or physically defend him from his captors, even though at one point he acknowledged that he could have summoned tens of thousands of angels to fight for him.

So not only do we see the humility of God in who Jesus was and what he did, we can also see that self-sacrificing (suffering) love is central to the way of Jesus. He referred to this as "laying down his life" for our sake in John 10. Echoing this phrasing, 1 John 3:16 says simply, "This is how we know what love is: Jesus Christ laid down his life for us." Jesus conquered sin and death by walking through them, not by physically overpowering or dominating them.

We are reminded of this every time we approach the communion table, every time we eat of the Lord's Supper. We receive and take bread and wine into our bodies as symbols of his body which he allowed to be broken for us. At his last meal with his disciples before his crucifixion, "he took bread, gave thanks and broke it, and gave it to them, saying, 'This is my body given for you; do this in remembrance of me.'" The broken bread of communion reminds us of his broken body.

"In the same way, after the supper he took the cup, saying, 'This cup is the new covenant in my blood, which is poured out for you'" (Luke 22:19-20). The communion cup reminds us of the blood he bled when he died. As Paul says, "whenever [we] eat this bread and drink this cup, [we] proclaim the Lord's death until he comes" (1 Cor. 11:26). Every observance of communion reminds us of God's self-sacrificing love for us made painfully clear in the obedience and loving humility of Jesus.

Following Jesus
Includes Following His Example

As followers of Jesus, Paul says we are called to live out the humility of God in our lives. Part of our mission is to reflect the nature and character of God, including his humility, like mirrors in the world. The point of the passage in Philippians 2, where Paul explains the humility of Jesus, is to provide the basis or rationale for why we should be humble. He tells us how humble Jesus was so that we will know what humility should look like in our lives.

> Don't be selfish; don't try to impress others. Be humble, thinking of others as better than yourselves. Don't look out only for your own interests, but take an interest in others, too. **You must have the same attitude that Christ Jesus had**. (Phil. 2:3-5, NLT)

This instruction isn't just some random commandment Paul thought up, as if he once thought, "Hmm, let's see, what can I tell them they have to do?" *No!* He is saying that following

Jesus means living as Jesus lived. Just as his mission was to reflect the nature and character of God to the world, so too our mission is the same. We are reconciled to God and to each other and empowered by the Holy Spirit so we can more faithfully reflect God to the world.

Jesus himself said it first. This idea was not original with Paul.

> Once when Jesus was praying in private and his disciples were with him, he asked them, "Who do the crowds say I am?" They replied, "Some say John the Baptist; others say Elijah; and still others, that one of the prophets of long ago has come back to life." "But what about you?" he asked. "Who do you say I am?" Peter answered, "God's Messiah." Jesus strictly warned them not to tell this to anyone. And he said, "The Son of man must suffer many things and be rejected by the elders, the chief priests and the teachers of the law, and he must be killed and on the third day be raised to life."
>
> Then he said to them all: **"Whoever wants to be my disciple must deny themselves and take up their cross daily and follow me.** For whoever wants to save their life will lose it, but whoever loses their life for me will save it. What good is it for someone to gain the whole world, and yet lose or forfeit their very self?" (Luke 9:18-25)

In short, if you want to follow me, you must follow my example. The death of Jesus "becomes the paradigm for an entirely new existence that is shaped ... by the cross. A life shaped by the cross is a life bent on dying daily to self to love God, self, others, and the world" (McKnight 2007, 69). This is a call to live out the same self-sacrificing, even suffering, love we saw Jesus live out. That kind of love is often uncomfortable, often costly, and sometimes excruciating. Whenever you offer this kind of love, it always feels as if some part of you is dying.

I omitted a crucial sentence when I quoted 1 John 3:16 above about Jesus laying down his life for us. The second part of the verse makes our point very specifically.

> This is how we know what love is: Jesus Christ laid down his life for us. And **we ought to lay down our lives for our brothers and sisters.** If anyone has material possessions and sees a brother or sister in need but has no pity on them, how can the love of God be in that person?
>
> Dear children, let us not love with words or speech but with actions and in truth. (1 John 3:16-18)

We learn what love is by learning what Jesus did. We saw true love defined by the actions of Jesus when he laid down his life for us. Following Jesus means following his example. As David Benner puts it,

> Christian spirituality is a path of descent, not ascent. Although we sometimes treat it as a spirituality of self-improvement through movement up a ladder of successive approximations to holiness, it is [actually] a spirituality of following Jesus on a journey of self-emptying.... Self-emptying is the core reality underlying every moment of Jesus' human journey. (Benner 2003, 99)

That is why Core Belief #6 is "We **surrender** our lives in love like Jesus did."

How Do We Do This?

How do we live out the humility of God in our lives?

How do we deny ourselves as Jesus did?

How do we reflect God's humility like mirrors in the world?

Let me first say, in the words of David Benner, that true Christian obedience is always grounded in our loving surrender to Jesus and made possible by the power of the Holy Spirit. It's not simply the acceptance of an obligation. The obedience we see in Jesus and which he has in mind for us "is surrender to love, not submission to a duty.... Christian obedience is more like what lovers give each other than what soldiers give their superiors." In other words, "We should obey God because he has won our hearts in love. If he has not, our focus should not be so much on obedience as on knowing his love. For once we get that solidly in place, obedience begins to take care of itself" (Benner 2003, 63).

With that in mind, let's revisit the four ways we said we saw humility and self-sacrificing (suffering) love lived out by Jesus and reframe them for our own lives.

1. First, ***we always invite people to follow Jesus***. We may even challenge them to do that, but we never demand or force people to follow Jesus or to agree with us, even when we are fully convinced that would be in their best interest. We never try to compel or coerce them to follow. We do not try to deceive them about this either. We love them, we live out and proclaim the truth, but we let them walk away if they are not yet ready to follow him, knowing that we each have to choose to follow Jesus in response to God's amazing love for us.

2. Second, by the transforming power of God at work within us, ***we interact with our opponents*** and our enemies with love, with grace, and with patience. We pray for them and hope for their (eventual?) flourishing in the life of the kingdom of God.

3. Third, ***we forgive the people who persecute us***, mistreat us, or wrong us. This is definitely not easy, but we seek to follow Jesus' example in obedience. We might clash with them and even challenge them sharply at times, but our aim is to reflect his loving humility in forgiving them.

4. Fourth, ***we are willing to suffer for the sake of the kingdom of God*** without retaliation. Following Jesus' example, we do not plot or scheme against anyone. We do not try to destroy our opponents and do not even really defend ourselves from them. "We suffer rather than force our way" (*Confession of Faith* 1995, 44). We believe Jesus calls us to love other people, even when it involves sacrifice or suffering.

We believe that loving our enemies, forgiving them, and not retaliating against them means rejecting violence as an option, just as Jesus did. We may challenge enemies, sometimes strongly, which Jesus did, too, but for their own good, always hoping to draw them toward living out the love of God, always hoping to help them 'Wake up!' to God's ways and purposes.

A caveat regarding abuse: This understanding of humility, surrender, and not retaliating against wrongdoers has sometimes been used by Christians to teach people to continue suffering physical, sexual, or emotional abuse in personal relationships and to continue to yield to their abusers. Let's be very clear about this. Your willingness to deny yourself and to suffer as a follower of Jesus does not mean you should let someone abuse you in personal relationships, especially in a dating or marriage relationship.

We are talking here about people who mistreat you for following Jesus and standing together in responding to them. If someone is abusing you, or if you think that may be happening, please speak up and get help.

I was deeply moved and profoundly inspired when I discovered the Alabama Christian Movement for Human Rights Pledge, written in Birmingham, Alabama, in 1963. Civil rights activists were asked to sign this Nonviolence Pledge as part of their training for joining the protest activities that challenged various racist policies and laws in their city.

Here (from Bhamwiki) are five of the ten commitments included in the pledge made by these very courageous brothers and sisters, a pledge that perfectly illustrates what it looks like to love, forgive, and not retaliate against our enemies.

1. MEDITATE daily on the teachings and life of Jesus.
2. REMEMBER always that the nonviolent movement seeks justice and reconciliation—not victory.
3. WALK and TALK in the manner of love, for God is love.
5. SACRIFICE personal wishes in order that all men might be free.
8. REFRAIN from the violence of fist, tongue, or heart.

In other words, following in the way of Jesus isn't going to be easy. It's going to cost you something, maybe quite a lot. Are you willing to sacrifice personal wishes (for example, to be safe, unharmed, fully employed) to bring about more justice for all of us?

Remember that we are pledged to nonviolent means and that our goal is justice and reconciliation rather than victory over our enemies. Our goal is a peaceful, free, and good life for ourselves rather than the punishment or destruction of the people who want to prevent us from living that way.

In prior chapters, we have noted two of the three themes Harold Bender highlighted in his *The Anabaptist Vision*—**reconciliation** as the core of the Christian faith (chapter 3) and **true community** as a central aspect of the life of God's people (chapter 6). Bender's third theme is **an ethic of "love and nonresistance** as applied to all human relationships" (Bender 1944, 31). This theme is closely related to the discussion of community in chapter 6 but has its deepest resonance here in our call to follow Jesus in humility and self-sacrificing love.

The Anabaptist emphasis on an ethic of love and nonresistance or nonviolence has been one of our most visible and distinctive practices over the centuries. Anabaptists were the first Christians in many centuries to reject violence and participation in warfare. This grew out of their profound embrace of the core beliefs reviewed in detail in earlier chapters. It isn't a separate belief that was added to the gospel. It's the natural outworking and integration of at least three of our core beliefs.

- See the sections on reconciliation, our ministry of reconciliation, citizens of two kingdoms, primary allegiance to Jesus Christ in chapter 3 on the kingdom.
- See the sections on nonconformity and whole-life discipleship in chapter 5 on following.
- See the discussion in this chapter on surrendering our lives in love like Jesus did.

By the power of the Holy Spirit at work within us, we are called to follow the example of the King of Kings and Lord of Lords (chapter 2 on Lordship) who laid down his life for his enemies rather than killing them.

Bender said the Anabaptists saw little chance that most people would ever embrace this perspective. Rather they "anticipated a long and grievous conflict between the church and the world" (because they are expressions of two very different kingdoms). Nor did they expect that the church would ever "rule the world; the church would always be a suffering church." On the other hand, "life within the Christian [community] is satisfyingly full of love and joy." That is because within the Christian community we can encourage each other and stand together in living out love and nonresistance, even when many people around us turn to conflict or violence. Our hope is to "practice what [Jesus] taught, believing that where he walked we can by his grace follow in his steps" (Bender 1944, 35-36).

5. A fifth way Anabaptists have sought to be faithful to the call and example of the humility of Jesus is by **maintaining a commitment to service**. We seek to serve. We want to be servant-hearted as Jesus was. This emphasis also comes directly from the words of Jesus. The Anabaptist tradition includes an ethos of service to each other, but also to people suffering from poverty, conflict, oppression, and disaster.

The gospel of Mark includes two brief stories about times when Jesus corrected his disciples for their lack of willingness to serve each other. In the first story, the disciples were arguing about which of them was the greatest as they walked along after Jesus. Jesus must have overheard them, because at some point he sat down and responded to their argument by saying, "Anyone who wants to be first must be the very last, and the servant of all" (Mark 9:34-35).

In the next chapter, two of Jesus' closest disciples, James and John, ask him to promise to give them preferential treatment in his coming kingdom. Mark does not tell us how Jesus felt about this request, but it's not hard to imagine that he might have been disappointed. In any case, he called his disciples together for another teaching moment, saying,

> "You know that those who are regarded as rulers of the Gentiles lord it over them, and their high officials exercise authority over them. Not so with you. Instead, whoever wants to become great among you **must be your servant**, and whoever wants to be first must be **slave of all. For even the Son of man did not come to be served, but to serve**, and to give his life as a ransom for many." (Mark 10:42-45)

Here again, Jesus reminds his followers of the example he has provided them and calls them to do what they have seen him do.

Peter emphasizes humility and service when he urges church leaders to

> Be shepherds of God's flock that is under your care, watching over them—not because you must, but because you are willing, as God wants you to be; not pursuing dishonest gain, but **eager to serve**; not lording it over those entrusted to you, but being examples to the flock.... All of you, **clothe yourselves with humility toward one another**, because, "God opposes the proud but shows favor to the humble." **Humble yourselves**, therefore, under God's mighty hand, that he may lift you up in due time. (1 Pet. 5:2-6)

So we seek to follow Jesus' example as a humble servant and to be examples ourselves to others.

Yieldedness

We see yet another expression of humility in the emphasis among the early Anabaptists on yieldedness (*Gelassenheit*) as a central and unifying theme for Christian discipleship. They called believers to yield within to the spirit of God, to yield outwardly to the Christian community and to the discipline or correction provided by that community, and beyond that to yield to God's will in how the surrounding world would treat them (Snyder 1995, 89).

Their embrace of this understanding of yieldedness enabled them to maintain a full surrender to the lordship of Jesus and to the will of God in the face of suffering, persecution, and martyrdom. They sought to be fully yielded to the will of God regardless of what it might cost them. They saw this as letting go of self-concern, letting go of things and people they treasured, and trusting that God was at work in them and would provide for them and their families.

Arnold Snyder points out that the key element of yieldedness is trust, a trust in God that leads to obedience and to a new way of living (Snyder 2004, 163). If you trust that God will provide for you, you can accept your circumstances with peace and grace. You can share your resources with people in need rather than stockpiling them, because you trust God to meet your needs in the future. And you can endure suffering, if need be, because you trust that God loves you and will give you and your loved ones what is needed. The early Anabaptists held that "only those who have practiced an active trust in God, who have experience in yielding themselves daily to God and the community, only such people will be able to withstand persecution, unto death" (Snyder 2004, 166).

Because this movement emerged in the face of intense persecution that too often ended in martyrdom, Anabaptists then and now talk about three baptisms. As noted in chapter 4, the first and essential baptism is our inner baptism with the Spirit. The second is our outer baptism with water which publicly announces our inner baptism. The third is our baptism in blood. For most of us, our first two baptisms simply express our willingness to experience the third one, but many of the early Anabaptists were literally baptized in the blood of suffering and death, following the example of their Lord Jesus.

Our *Confession of Faith* says,

> Baptism is done in obedience to Jesus' command and as a public commitment to identify with Jesus Christ, not only in his baptism by water, but in his life in the Spirit, and in his death in suffering love.... Those who accept water baptism commit themselves to follow Jesus in living their lives for others, in loving their enemies, and in renouncing violence, even when it means their own suffering or death. (*COF* 1995, 46-47)

This is another reason why we don't baptize young children. We don't consider them capable of understanding or handling the profound implications of driving a car or of committing themselves to marriage. Yet the implications of a commitment to whole life discipleship that includes a willingness to suffer and die are even more profound. It's only when they are a bit older that they can grasp the wide-ranging implications of surrendering their lives to Jesus as described in the New Testament and make an informed choice to do that.

Foot Washing

Jesus provided us with a simple ritual to remind us of our commitment to reflect his loving humility in our time. Our *Confession of Faith* says, "In washing his disciples' feet, Jesus acted out a parable of his life unto death for them, and of the way his disciples are called to live in the world" (*COF* 1995, 53).

Foot washing was a common practice in first-century Palestine where people wore sandals and walked dusty roads every day. Normally, people washed their own feet. In a household, a servant or slave might wash the master's feet. Occasionally, a disciple might wash the feet of his teacher as an act of extraordinary devotion. *No one* would *ever* have expected Jesus, the master, to wash his disciples' feet.

On the evening before he was arrested, and after a meal with his disciples, Jesus *completely stunned* them by kneeling down behind them as they reclined at the table and by proceeding to wash their feet. It would have been strange enough to have another disciple washing their feet, but it was awkward in the extreme to have their revered leader and teacher do so. It would have taken him awhile to wash the feet of twelve men—I am guessing at least ten to fifteen minutes. They means they probably had at least that much time to squirm in the baffled discomfort Peter expressed for all of them.

When Jesus finally finished washing their feet, I think he stunned them again when he said to them, "Since I, your Lord and Teacher, have washed your feet, you ought to wash each other's feet. I have given you an example to follow. Do [for each other] as I have done for you" (John 13:14-15).

On top of all the other ways Jesus expressed his humility and his self-sacrificing love, he once actually knelt down and did something that only a servant would have done. And then he said very clearly, I want you to follow my example. I want you to love and serve each other the way I have loved and served you.

Christians disagree about whether he meant "you ought to wash each other's feet" as a literal or symbolic instruction. You can look it up. The Greek words literally read, "you also ought to wash one another's feet." Anabaptists/ Mennonites have chosen to receive this instruction both literally and symbolically, because in literally washing each other's feet, we symbolically recommit ourselves to:

Humility—to following the example of Jesus who humbled himself in taking on human form and in submitting to death on the cross. When you kneel before your brother or sister in Christ and wash their feet, you remind them, yourself, and God that you are humbling yourself before God and before his purposes for your life.

Service—to following the example of Jesus who gave up his privileges and his life to serve us. When you kneel before your brother or sister in Christ to wash her or his feet, you remind them, yourself, and God that you are willing to serve God, this particular person, and by extension your brothers and sisters in Christ. By kneeling and washing, you demonstrate that you are a servant who is willing to carry out God's assignments for you even if they are not always convenient for you.

Reconciliation—Washing each other's feet reminds us that our reconciliation with God is expressed in our ongoing reconciliation with each other. A foot-washing service is a great time to seek someone out, to be reconciled with them, and then to express that reconciliation through foot washing. It does not all have to happen in that moment, but the activity of foot washing expresses your commitment to be reconciled.

Washing each other's feet is a very simple, very concrete way to demonstrate and to reflect the loving humility of God.

Story: Alternative Service

In chapter 5, I told the story of the villagers of Eyam in 1665 as an example of discipleship in action (of following Jesus in everyday life). That story is also a terrific example of "surrendering our lives in love like Jesus did." Here is another story that illustrates humility and service motivated by Christians' desire to follow the example of Jesus in specific situations.

Mennonites and other Anabaptists have been known for their refusal to participate in warfare between nations since their beginning in the early 1500s. This commitment has been tested in various ways for Mennonites who live in what is now the United States ever since they began immigrating in the late

1600s. For example, during World War 1 the federal government made no provision for conscientious objection to military service. Men claiming to be conscientious objectors (COs) were court-martialed and imprisoned. They reported being cursed, beaten, kicked, and compelled to exercise to the point of physical collapse. Others were underfed, put in solitary confinement, or forced to do hard physical labor. In at least two cases, the treatment was so severe that the men died from it.

By the time of World War 2, the peace churches (the three oldest pacifist denominations in the U.S.: Quaker/Friends, Mennonite, Church of the Brethren) and the federal government had worked together to develop an alternative to military service for COs called Civilian Public Service (CPS). CPS workers were assigned to do "work of national importance" in lieu of military service. They fought forest fires, worked in mental institutions, planted trees, did dairy testing, and served as subjects for medical experiments motivated by military interests. For example, some volunteered to be subjects in studies of the impact of starvation or sleeplessness or extreme temperatures on the human body. Others agreed to be infected with typhus, malaria, or hepatitis so immunologists could test various treatments for these diseases.

Conditions in the mental hospitals often shocked and dismayed the men who worked in them. They were troubled by violence against and general disregard for the patients. Many of them worked as orderlies—changing sheets, feeding patients, and wheeling them to electric shock treatments in twelve hour shifts, six days a week—so they were deeply involved with the care of patients, confronting the sights, the smells, and the sounds of a hidden-away part of society on a daily basis.

Some of them brought hidden cameras into the hospitals to document what they were experiencing. When a selection of these photographs was published along with an exposé in a May 1946 edition of *Life* magazine, they provoked a national reaction and calls for change.

In the years that followed, as the CPS workers returned home after the war, they talked together about what they could do to provide more professional and more humane care for mentally ill patients. Some enrolled in medical training programs. Others helped to organize mental health facilities run by Mennonites in Maryland, Pennsylvania, California, Kansas, and Indiana. Their determination to provide better care for defenseless and discarded people helped to initiate large-scale changes in this part of the medical field.

In *If We Can Love: The Mennonite Mental Health Story*, Vernon Neufeld wrote,

> No other church group had ever had such a concentrated experience with mental illness as the American Mennonites during World War II. [Out of that experience, they] developed a vision of what might be done with rightly motivated psychiatric aides and mental health professionals. (Neufeld 1983, 26)

Their commitment to nonresistance, humility, and service (as a way of surrendering their lives in love like Jesus did) profoundly shaped their experience of and reflections on their time in CPS and extended well beyond it.

It's Not Easy to Live This Way!

This core belief is the one that is most likely to sound completely backwards or upside down to many American Christians, especially when we realize that "taking up my cross" does not just mean being willing to wait my turn or be respectful to people I disagree with or being content with what I have.

All of those are fine as far as they go, but it's much more disturbing to realize that "taking up my cross" means being willing to be humiliated, willing to suffer, even willing to die if that is what it costs us to follow Jesus and to obey his call on our lives. We Americans are more used to being told we need to stand up for our rights, to fight for our rights, or even to make our opponents (and especially our enemies) pay for the ways they have intruded on our lives or failed to respect our rights! We are more likely to be told that if necessary, we may have to force people we disagree with to do what we think is right.

I heard Pastor Scott Sauls say in an interview in a "Happy Hour with Jame Ivey Podcast" (and included in Sauls' *A Gentle*

Answer, Nelson, 2020) that "The American dream is to deny my neighbor, take up my comforts, and follow my dreams, whereas the way of Jesus is to deny myself, take up my cross, follow my Lord, and let him reshape my dreams."

Of course, Americans are not the only ones to struggle with Jesus' call to surrender our lives in love like he did. We saw in chapter 3 that Kenyan Christians killed each other in 2007 when their tribal loyalties pitted them against each other. The same was true during the 1994 genocide in Rwanda. We saw that the same thing happened in World War 1 among Christians in Western Europe.

American Christians from many denominations, including some Mennonites and other Anabaptists, have been and continue to be drawn into passionate embrace of militarism, nationalism, redemptive violence, and enraged political polarization permeating public culture in the U.S. It's not easy to continue to resist all of this when it's everywhere we turn.

But this is also not really a new development. For example, during the American Civil War most of the combatants would have claimed Christian faith. This struggle has just taken on new forms. Conscientious objectors have been scorned and vilified in each of the U.S.'s major wars. Of the 9809 Mennonites who were drafted into military service between 1940 and 1947, 54 percent chose military service rather than Civilian Public Service (CPS)—even though CPS options were well planned and readily available. As many as two thirds of the men who chose military service did not return to the Mennonite church after serving, including several of my great-uncles. On the other hand, almost none of the men who were drafted from the Amish served in the military.

When we read the Philippians 2 passage about the humility of Jesus, we are probably most inspired by Jesus' triumph in verses 9-11. There we learn that God "exalted him to the highest place and gave him the name that is above every name, that at the name of Jesus every knee should bow, in heaven and on earth and under the earth."

As Philippians celebrates that every tongue will "acknowledge that Jesus Christ is Lord, to the glory of God the Father," we revel in his lordship over absolutely everything and everyone. We're relieved that he finally has power over them and can make them do what he wants them to do. We're convinced that he wants to use that power to make *our* opponents do what *we* want them to do. We forget that he is qualified to be Lord over absolutely everything *because of* his loving humility and surrender (obedience) to the mission of God to reconcile all things to himself. That is who he is and who he will continue to be. And he calls us to follow his example.

Revelation chapter 5 announces Jesus as the Lion of the tribe of Judah, prompting us to raise our fists in triumph and let out a cheer. It turns out, however, that when John turns his head to look at this lion, what he sees is a lamb who looks as if he has been violently killed (Rev. 5:6). He does not see a powerful animal roaring in the angry flush of victory. He sees the smallest and mildest animal, who does not say or do anything other than simply stand at the center of the throne and receive the worship of everyone around him. Yes, he is the triumphant hero, but he does not look like any other triumphant hero we have ever encountered or imagined.

Here we confront again the distinction between the kingdoms of God and of the world—the two kingdoms shaped by different values, different methods, and different goals. As followers of Jesus, we are citizens of the kingdom of God first and citizens of the kingdom(s) of the world second. The way we function in the particular kingdom of the world where we live will be limited by our surrender to the values, methods, and goals of the kingdom of God. We look to the example of the life and teachings of Jesus for how to navigate the tension of our dual citizenship. We seek to reflect his example in our lives and in our time.

It's clear from the life and teachings of Jesus that we are called to love other people, even when that involves sacrifice or suffering. It's also clear that we are called to humility and service to be faithful to the call and example of Jesus. Anabaptists understand that call to include a rejection of violence (a call to nonresistance), since we see no way to fit a call to violence into the example of Jesus nor with his call to reconciliation, love, sacrifice, suffering, humility, and service. This is not a popular stance in any nation's public culture; it's also not even the majority view among Christians, so it really isn't easy to live this way.

Summary

Surrendering our lives in love like Jesus did (core belief #6) is grounded in the humility of God, which we understand much more clearly because of the example and teachings of Jesus. In his life and example, we see but struggle to grasp the astonishing cost to himself that God has been willing to pay to reconcile all things to himself.

Jesus then astonished his followers by calling them to follow his example. This astonishes us even today. It's one thing to watch someone else do unimaginably daring things; it's quite another thing to then be challenged to follow in their steps and do what they just did. But that is precisely what Jesus did when he gave his disciples a simple but utterly life-changing command to "love each other as I have loved you." He explained that what he meant was that we should lay down our lives for each other in humility and service just as he did for us. Anabaptists believe that call extends to all of us who follow him today.

It turns out that one of the main purposes of Jesus' mission in coming to live among us was to empower us to live the life of love, humility, and service that he lived. He didn't seem to care that that would make his followers unusual no matter where they lived. Quite the opposite. He expected their example to draw other people into the kingdom of God. He also said the people around you will know you are my followers *because* of how you love each other.

In this chapter, we looked at the examples of foot washing and the CPS workers who sought to provide more professional and more humane care for the mentally ill. These are two ways Christians have looked very different from others because of their willingness to surrender their lives in love like Jesus did.

NOTE: You can read more about the themes covered in this chapter in the following articles of the Confession of Faith in a Mennonite Perspective –*10: The church in mission, 11: Baptism, 12: The Lord's Supper, 13: Foot Washing, 17: Discipleship and the Christian Life, 18: Christian Spirituality, 22: Peace, Justice, and Nonresistance.*

Chapter 8

Practices Based on the Core Beliefs

In late 1568 or early 1569, Dirk Willems was arrested as a heretic in his hometown of Asperen in what is now the Netherlands. Willems was likely born Catholic, but he became an Anabaptist when he was rebaptized as an adult. Unfortunately, he lived during the time when local officials under the Duke of Alba (who would have considered himself a Christian) were tracking down and executing people considered to be heretics, so Willems was arrested, convicted, and imprisoned for his faith.

After at least several months in the castle prison that winter, Willems escaped by lowering himself from a window with a rope made of knotted rags and dropping onto the ice that covered the castle moat. The prison guards spotted him as he fled and chased him. As he headed out across a nearby pond, which was also covered with ice, his pursuers followed.

Partway across the pond, his main pursuer broke through the ice and fell into the freezing water. Willems didn't break through the ice himself, in part because he was a smaller person than the guard, but also because he had been living on prison rations for several months and had lost weight. When he heard the guard's cries for help, Willems turned back and helped the man clamber back up onto the surface of the ice.

The man he rescued was grateful and knew he owed his life to Willems. He wanted to let him go, but the local official on the scene reminded him of the oath he had taken to uphold the law and ordered him to seize Willems. He reluctantly obeyed and led Willems back to captivity.

This time Willems was put into a small, heavily barred room at the top of a tall church tower above the steeple bell. His legs were probably locked into the wooden stocks that are still there today. On May 16, 1569, Dirk Willems was burned at the stake for being a heretic, described by one of his judges as being obstinately persistent in his beliefs (Braght 1951, 741).

This amazing story illustrates how our core beliefs shape our behavior. All involved in capturing, imprisoning, condemning, and finally executing Dirk Willems would have considered themselves Christians. They would probably have seen what they were doing as necessary and good, because they were upholding the law and defending the true Christian faith, even if the way it all worked out was somewhat unsettling.

If not a Jesus-focused Anabaptist, Willems might have seen his pursuer's misfortune and death as reenacting the crossing of the Red Sea, when the Egyptians were drowned as part of God's deliverance of his people from their enemies. He might have happily continued on his way singing Miriam's song to celebrate the way God had miraculously rescued him.

But Willems's imagination was more deeply shaped by Jesus' example of surrendering his life in love. He was surrendered to the lordship of Jesus, seeking to follow him in daily life and humbly surrendering his life in love like Jesus did. He remembered what Jesus taught and modeled about loving our enemies. He knew that Jesus gave his life for his enemies rather than taking their lives to protect himself, and he knew that Jesus called his followers, including Willems, to do the same.

He could not have known exactly what would follow rescuing his pursuer, but he must have known he was risking his life to save the very man trying to capture and return him to prison. As it turned out, he saved the life of his pursuer at the cost of his own life and the agony of a physically excruciating death.

It's hard to imagine that you or I would do what Willems did with only seconds to decide and act. Our imaginations are so deeply formed by individualism (my well-being and my rights are centrally important, I should defend myself), victory for me (one of God's main jobs is to make sure I don't come to harm), and redemptive violence (the best way to deal with enemies is to destroy them), that it might not even occur to us to worry about what would happen to our pursuer. How long would it take for us to realize that Jesus might have some guidance for us in a situation like this one? We might not even realize what our true core beliefs were until it was all over, when we reviewed what happened and tried to make sense of our response. Willems probably didn't know that he would risk his life to save his enemy (that he would lay down his life in loving and serving his enemy) until he faced this moment of crisis.

Of course, this story also reminds us of the tension I mentioned in chapter 7. On the one hand, we are called to surrender our lives in love like Jesus did. That core belief provides a helpful way to understand what Willems did and is why I include it here. On the other hand we might ask: At what point does a willingness to surrender or yield to other people cross the line into allowing ourselves to be abused? How do we distinguish between persecution and abuse? I do not offer Willems's action as the primary example for how to respond to someone who is abusive.

This tension is real and important but takes us beyond the scope of this book. Let me simply note that we see this same tension in Jesus' ministry. There were times when Jesus moved out of or stayed out of harm's way (e.g., Luke 4:29-30, John 7:1, 10, 30), but there were other times when he suffered a great deal. When Jesus suffered, his underlying trust was in God's wisdom, love, and care, but he did not simply allow his enemies to injure or mistreat him whenever and however they wanted.

My larger point in telling Willems's story is that whether you realize it or not, your behavior is shaped by your core beliefs, too. Some combination of the ideas and habits and attitudes you grew up with, your reflection on and reaction to them, and your current influences have shaped your beliefs about what is and is not important in life. Those beliefs shape the way you think, speak, dress, spend your time, spend your money, treat other people, and even what you think is funny. They also shape the way you make sense of the world around you, the way you read or do not read the Bible, and the way you do or do not follow Jesus.

All of that is also true for Anabaptists. Having embraced and committed ourselves to the six core beliefs, we find they provide a way of understanding the world around us, of reading the Bible, and of responding to Jesus. They help us decide what is and is not important and shape the way we think, speak, dress, spend our time and money, treat other people, and even what we think is or is not funny. Over time, our core beliefs and the way they shape our behavior settles into habits. We can refer to the habits we develop as "practices."

Here is a reminder of the six core beliefs.

1. **Jesus is Lord** over absolutely everything.
2. The **kingdom of God** is where people unite under the lordship of Jesus.
3. We **choose** to follow Jesus.
4. We **follow** Jesus in everyday life.
5. We follow Jesus **together.**
6. We **surrender our lives in love** like Jesus did.

These six Anabaptist core beliefs lead us to a wholehearted, whole-life surrender to the lordship of Jesus that shapes our approach to every aspect of our everyday lives in the real world. They shape our practices (our behaviors which become habits), so this isn't just a spiritual experience that takes place mostly in our minds or our emotions or in the spiritual realm. It's a lived, visible surrender that changes everything. We're willing, by the power of the Holy Spirit at work within us, to adjust or change anything about our lives, our habits, our thoughts, our commitments, or our behaviors to obey the call of Jesus to look more like him and to more faithfully live the life he has called us to.

We acknowledge that we are not the primary focus of our lives, Jesus is. The kingdom of God is our focus. At our best, we are also more likely than most Americans to yield to or cooperate with our local body of believers.

Anabaptist Practices
Express Anabaptist Core Beliefs

The practices of the various Anabaptist groups (Mennonites, Amish, Hutterites, Brethren) have historically been most of what other Christians know about Anabaptist life and thought.

They stand out because several of them are not widely shared by other Christians. As such, our practices have sometimes been mistaken for core beliefs, even by Anabaptists themselves. Many people seem to have the impression that Anabaptists have simply selected practices like nonresistance or foot washing or humility from a "Ways to Be Unusual" catalog, leaving everyone else to wonder why they would do that and failing to realize that all of us are expressing our core beliefs in our practices of daily living.

All of the practices that you think of as particular (or peculiar) to Anabaptists are in some way grounded in our core beliefs and in this way of thinking and living. In earlier chapters, I explained the background to Anabaptist practices like mutual aid, church as loving community, foot washing, nonconformity, nonresistance (nonviolence), wearing plain clothing, yieldedness, and baptizing believers rather than infants. I linked each of these practices to an underlying core belief.

None of these practices are ends in themselves. Each points back to and gives concrete form to some combination of the six core beliefs that give meaning to and provide a rationale for the practices. Each of the practices is then shaped by a particular cultural setting and point in time. For example, what are the mechanisms by which a particular congregation provides mutual aid? How will they do foot washing? What do nonconformity or nonresistance look like for this congregation? How do they prepare people for baptism and then baptize them?

Here are several more examples of Anabaptist practices and the core beliefs they express. Remember that these practices are not core beliefs or core values in and of themselves. They are *expressions* of core beliefs. They are specific ways various Anabaptists have chosen to make the core beliefs real and visible in shaping their everyday lives.

Not Swearing Oaths, Truth Telling, Simplicity, Good Stewardship, Witness in Word and Deed

All of these are seen as obeying the simple, direct commands of Jesus, drawing largely on the Sermon on the Mount in

Matthew 5-7. Jesus calls us to be honest and truthful. He calls us to have enough integrity that people believe and trust us when we say Yes or No. We should not have to swear an oath to convince people that we will now tell the truth. Jesus calls us not to worry about clothing or food or adornment. He calls us to honor God in every aspect of our lives.

Jesus cared about people's bodies and livelihoods and spiritual journeys. Yes, he called them to repent of their sins but also knew they needed health, food, ways to make a living, and freedom from oppression and exploitation. He said we would be judged in part on the basis of how well we care for "the least of these." For Anabaptists, such concerns have been part of seeing the kingdom of God come to life as all are able to flourish in God's purposes for them and for the world. We don't pit caring for physical needs against caring for spiritual needs, understanding that both of them are a focus in the kingdom of God.

Underlying core beliefs

#2. A joyful embrace of the coming of the kingdom of God as the focus of God's mission in the world.

#4. A serious commitment to follow Jesus in everyday life, obeying his commands and following his example for how to live our lives (discipleship).

#6. Surrendering our lives in love means living in loving humility and being willing to serve other people, helping to meet their needs and helping them experience the love of God through both what we say and what we do.

Church Discipline

Church discipline was an early Anabaptist hallmark practice. As we saw in chapter 5 in the discussion of discipleship, one of the main drivers of this movement was dismay at the lack of changed lives among people considered to be fine Christians. The early Anabaptists knew something was wrong in the church when supposed followers of Jesus behaved in completely contrary ways to most of how he called his followers to live.

They corrected members who were falling back into sinful habits to help those members find freedom from sin and to protect the integrity of the church's shared witness in teaching and in holy living. This is still understood by Anabaptists as part of providing mutual care for each other in the church as we give and receive guidance on what faithful discipleship looks like (*Confession of Faith* 1995, 55).

The early Anabaptists didn't discipline problematic members with the weapons or the power of the government as other reformers were doing. They argued strongly for limiting church discipline to confrontation, reproof, withholding communion, and eventually withholding relationship (banning or shunning) or full separation (excommunication), and they practiced all of these things. The goal was to protect the unity of the church and to restore erring members to the fellowship of the church.

Church discipline is not usually very complicated or controversial when the issue is something like adultery or drunkenness or lying. I know a man who committed adultery whose marriage and ministry were eventually restored as a result of his wholehearted cooperation with church discipline for about five years. Church leaders were loving but firm with him in designing a process for repentance, counseling, and mentoring. He fully complied with what they asked of him, and his life was transformed. I know other people in related situations who have resisted correction, but their removal from positions of responsibility has provided protection for the congregation.

Anabaptists' core beliefs of following Jesus together (core belief 5) and yielding to each other (part of core belief 6) have meant that we have often attempted to come to shared agreements about lifestyle practices. Church discipline is much more challenging when the issue is a failure to comply with shared understandings or directives for how to practice simplicity or which worship practices are acceptable. In this type of situation, leaders and mature believers have sometimes disagreed with each other on whom to discipline and which infractions require which kind of discipline. These disagreements have too often escalated to the point of splitting the group and wounding the people or the group of people being disciplined, especially among Mennonites, and especially when the discipline was seen to be harsh or heartless.

For example, this was the main source of the separation of the Amish from the Mennonites. In 1693, a determined Mennonite elder named Jacob Amman gathered a group of Mennonites, mostly located in the Alsace region in the easternmost part of today's France, who wanted the church to enforce a stricter set of expectations for uniformity of dress and appearance (like untrimmed beards for men). He advocated strongly for excommunicating and shunning members who didn't comply, but his detractors thought he was rash and too harsh, especially when he excommunicated all the Mennonite elders and bishops who disagreed with him.

None of the later attempts to reconcile the differences between his followers and the larger group succeeded. Amman's followers came to be known as "Amish Mennonites." They largely retain the dress, customs, and language of the Alsace region from about 1700 to the present day and are now simply known as "Amish."

Examples from the 1900s include excommunications over the introduction of Sunday school classes and how to respond to Mennonite men who joined the military. Some of the descendants and congregations of people who were disciplined on these matters still carry emotional and spiritual wounds from the experiences of their forebears. In most of these cases, the people being disciplined saw themselves as legitimate dissenters from a misguided policy, and the wounding resulted from the severity and the inflexibility of the enforcement.

The hope is that church discipline will help erring members see their actions from the perspective of their brothers and sisters in Christ, yield to the correction, and be restored to fellowship (see Matt. 18:15-20). Yet this is sometimes very hard to do.

The concern for living holy lives and the church's responsibility to discipline wayward members led many Anabaptist groups to "take counsel" before serving communion. Taking Paul's admonition in 1 Corinthians 11 not to participate in communion in an "unworthy manner," either because of sin or disunity in the body, the communion ceremony was preceded by an opportunity to evaluate one's relationships with God and with other members of the body.

In some cases, this was accomplished by scheduling a special preparatory service, often on either a Saturday or Sunday, the week before communion would be served. Leaders would review the passage from 1 Corinthians 11 and remind members to resolve any matters of sin or broken relationships either during the preparatory service or sometime before the following Sunday. Framed in this way, the tone of communion services was often fairly solemn because members feared the consequences of participating unworthily.

Underlying core beliefs

#4. A serious commitment to follow Jesus in everyday life (discipleship) and a willingness to behave differently from non-Christians (nonconformity).

#5. Following Jesus together and #6. Surrendering our lives in love shaped a willingness to make shared decisions about how to live in the world and to yield oneself (yieldedness) to those shared decisions.

What About Legalism?

Keep in mind that all of these Anabaptist practices are only meaningful as expressions of the six core beliefs. If we disconnect the practices from their sources in the core beliefs, we lose the meanings of and reasons for the practices.

When an Anabaptist group has defined faithful discipleship as yielding to and adopting certain practices (like the Rules and Disciplines documents drawn up by Lancaster Mennonite Conference or the ban on Sunday school described above), people who dissent from the practices have sometimes come to see the Anabaptist/Mennonite perspective as something added to basic Christian discipleship that's not actually necessary or that goes beyond scriptural teaching. They see and experience the emphasis on uniformity in specific practices as legalism.

The irony, of course, is that at its best the Anabaptist/ Mennonite perspective is an attempt to be as rigorously faithful as possible to the New Testament. The goal has always been to live out nothing more and nothing less than the plain and simple teachings of Jesus.

For example, in the early 1970s, the Rules and Disciplines required women being baptized in Lancaster Mennonite Conference congregations to begin wearing a head (prayer) covering of a certain style once they were baptized and therefore members of the church. Some young women who wanted to be baptized but not begin wearing a "covering" delayed their baptisms despite the mounting pressure of expectations and concerns about their salvation. However well intentioned, an insistence on the wearing of a specific "covering" as a condition for baptism came to be seen by some as an embrace of legalism.

In some cases, the insistence on specific practices was so unrelenting that people who wanted more flexibility or freedom regarding the practices felt as if a.) church membership (and by implication right-standing with God) was being defined more by compliance with the practices than by affirmation of the core beliefs, and b.) they faced an either-or decision—either comply with these particular practices or leave the church. Some eventually relented but others left.

Because many Anabaptist congregations tended to be close-knit communities up until the second half of the twentieth century, leaving them meant disrupting a whole network of relationships and being frowned on as being contentious and headstrong. It's not hard to imagine that many dissenters saw the congregations they left as legalistic. In some cases, rejection of the practices included a full rejection of the underlying core beliefs either as meaningless or as the source of the legalism they were trying to escape. In other cases, people were able to hold onto the core beliefs, distinguishing between them and the particular set of practices they wanted to leave behind.

Some Anabaptist Practices Reflect Swiss German Culture

Since one of the main places Anabaptist thought first emerged was in the German-speaking part of Switzerland, many Anabaptist practices were also shaped by Swiss German culture.

The early Anabaptists were responding to the challenges of their place and time just as you and I do today. In the early 1500s, new and direct access to the Scriptures began inspiring

Christians in what are now Switzerland, Germany, Austria, The Netherlands, and France to rethink their theology and practice. The Anabaptists sprang from groups that wanted to reconsider everything. Their vision for change is still considered radical in the sense that it was all-encompassing and much more thorough-going than most other reformers were willing to consider.

For example, they didn't see any scriptural basis for letting governments make decisions about what would be permitted in the worship and practices of the church, no matter how well intentioned. They were dismayed that people, including priests, who were considered Christians in good standing by their local churches were living sinful lives and that no one seemed concerned that they showed few signs of being regenerated by the work of the Holy Spirit. They also believed that state officials who claimed to be Christian yet used the weapons and power of the state to enforce theological beliefs and practices derived from such beliefs were profoundly violating the teachings and spirit of Jesus.

The church of their time seemed to them to have wandered far from the picture of the kingdom of God provided by Jesus and his apostles in the New Testament. They were frustrated that other reformers seemed content with a partial rather than complete reformation of the church. They were especially dismayed that the other reformers had no interest in disentangling the power and weapons of the state from the life of the church.

They wanted to start over as much as possible by rethinking the teachings and practices of the church based on the New Testament and the clear call of Jesus to follow his example and teachings. So they began baptizing believers rather than infants, emphasizing true life change, and refusing to participate in warfare. They found the basis for all three of these actions in the New Testament but were also motivated to emphasize these practices by the challenges they faced in their time and place.

The early Anabaptist immigrants to what are now the United States and Canada largely came from this cultural group. Some of them migrated to Germany, others to Russia (mostly in what is now Ukraine), before they made their way to the New World. Many of them had turned to farming as a way to avoid attracting too much notice in the places they settled. So by the time they arrived in the New World, they settled in largely agrarian areas—rural areas outside Philadelphia and Lancaster County, Pennsylvania, and later the rural areas in Ontario and the plains of the U.S. and Canada. In most cases, they arrived as German-speaking immigrants as closely connected to each other by family ties as by their faith.

In the eastern U.S., especially in Lancaster County, where I live, and some surrounding counties in Pennsylvania, it has been common for even Mennonites themselves to confuse Swiss German culture (cultural habits) with what it means to "be Mennonite." Swiss Germans tend to be hard working, exacting, frugal, quiet, and conflict-averse. Because most Mennonites in Lancaster County have been Swiss German, any who do not have a recognizably German last name still risk being told, "That's not a Mennonite name!" when introducing themselves in a Mennonite congregation. As if there were such a thing. What the speaker really means is "That's not a *Swiss-German* name."

Swiss Germans are also often not very demonstrative, so Mennonites from other ethnic groups are left to wonder why Swiss Germans are so reluctant to raise their hands or shout in church. Unfortunately, Swiss Germans also too often respond to conflict in passive-aggressive ways. But such Swiss German tendencies have little to do with "being Mennonite" as they are not based on the six core values. They are the cultural habits of a particular group of people.

Another example is the dress and grooming styles of the Amish. I still remember my astonishment when I discovered mannequins in a cultural museum in Europe dressed very much like my Amish neighbors. The displays in the museum portrayed the cultural styles and patterns in that area across the centuries. I realized that the Amish hadn't simply made up these styles to express their convictions. They have simply preserved the dress and grooming styles of a particular time and place, which turns out to be the Alsace region from about 1700.

The lives and thoughts of Anabaptists in or from Latin America or Africa or Asia are also shaped by their particular cultural settings. For example, worship in Latin America and in Africa is generally far more expressive, worship in Africa often includes group dancing, and few Anabaptists from any of these parts of the world would have a Swiss German last name.

No Acultural Christian Life

Some Christians, especially Christians trying to move beyond the confines of legalism, ask, "Can't I just be a Christian? Should we not try to rid ourselves of all the trappings of culture and denomination?" That sounds so appealing.

But in short, no. There is no such thing as acultural Christianity, that is, a Christian faith that's not lived out in a particular time and place and among a particular group of people. Our faith is an incarnated faith. It has to be seen and expressed in the everyday lives of real people. The good news of Jesus is meant to be communicated in each new culture it reaches in ways that are true both to the message and to the cultural setting. Local expressions of the kingdom of God are going to be flavored a bit differently in different cultural settings.

Core beliefs like discipleship or loving community or yieldedness only have their intended meaning if you live them out in some way within a particular cultural setting, in a particular time and place, and among a particular group of people. You have to translate your core beliefs into behavioral practices for them to become real. They won't match their descriptions in the New Testament if they exist only in your mind or your intentions. You and other people have to see them expressed or lived out in concrete, specific ways.

Over time, Christians in each cultural group develop habits about how they live out their faith. They develop rhythms for what following Jesus looks like in their particular setting. For example, every Christian group has to make decisions about how to worship, how to talk about and serve communion, how to talk about and administer baptism, and about how to relate to each other in the congregation—in ways that are faithful both to the way of Jesus and to the cultural setting.

All of those decisions are shaped by a.) our (theological) understanding of the meaning and importance of these things and b.) our previous experience of how these things were explained and carried out in other times and places. The only way to have a culture-free Christian life would be to never make these decisions, and to never develop habits or rhythms for following Jesus together.

This also means that every Christian faith community (every congregation) has a personality—including things like a way (habits) of expressing emotion, a way (habits) of treating each other, a way (habits) of responding to conflict. You can sense these habits and the overall personality of the group when you visit them even if no one says anything about how the group deals with emotions, relationships, or conflicts.

We should also remember that we are all creatures of habit. We get used to doing things a certain way, in part so we don't have to constantly remake all of our decisions about worship (style, order of service), about fellowship, about communion, or about baptism. Even non-liturgical and non-denominational churches develop habits about these things. The practices of non-denominational churches are shaped by the leaders' theological understanding, by the leaders' previous experiences, and by their sense of either the "right" way to do these things or at least the range of 'acceptable' ways to do these things. Their ideas about these things are shaped directly by the habits and practices of the Christian groups or congregations they have previously known or have, in some cases, reacted against. It's simply not humanly possible to live the Christian life or to function as a congregation without developing any habits for how you do it.

Anabaptist Christians are no different. If our practices look different or unusual to you, it's simply because you either have a different theological understanding of their meaning and importance or your previous experience of the Christian journey has been shaped by a different set of habits.

Since culture, in a broad sense, is simply the collection of habits people develop and share as they live together, different groups of Christians, including Anabaptists, will develop different habits about how they live out (how they express) their core beliefs in specific practices. So Swiss German Anabaptists will develop practices that make sense to them in their broader cultural setting. Russian Anabaptists practices will make sense to them in their broader cultural settings. Likewise their settings will shape practices of Ethiopians, Tanzanians, Indonesians, and every other people group where Anabaptist (or any other Christian) theology and core beliefs take root.

Over time and across generations, it's easy to begin confusing practices with beliefs. If preachers and teachers don't clearly and regularly distinguish between the two and explain how the practices they advocate are grounded in specific beliefs, their congregants are likely to forget the connection. They will forget why they are being asked to carry out the practices. That's when people come to believe "this is just how we do it" or when the practices start to be seen as ends in themselves. Neither of these is the rationale Jesus provides for following him in everyday life.

Summary

We can't help it. It's just part of the human condition. We are creatures of habit, and the behavioral habits we develop (our practices) express our core beliefs. Whether you realize it or not, the way you live your life flows directly from what you truly believe. The good news is that we have the capacity to choose our core beliefs and which behavior habits to adopt. Followers of Jesus are especially able to do this because of the power of the Holy Spirit at work within us.

Over the centuries, Anabaptists have identified a wide range of shared practices that flow from our core beliefs. These practices are how we make our core beliefs real in our everyday lives, and we adapt them to specific cultural settings. We reviewed several in earlier chapters, and I presented a few more in this chapter.

We create two problems when the distinction between our core beliefs and our practices isn't clear. First, we may treat our practices as core beliefs themselves. A good example of this confusion in Mennonite history is when people treat peace or nonresistance as our primary aim rather than grounding our commitment to that practice in the example, teaching, and work of Jesus. When we treat peace as a core belief, we forget that we seek to be people of peace because that's what Jesus calls us to. We forget that we didn't choose to follow Jesus because we were first committed to peace (as an end in itself), and then we found Jesus to be its best or most compelling advocate.

The second problem is that we lose the connections of the practices to the underlying core beliefs. We forget the rationale for the practices; they just become our habits. We're no longer entirely sure why they *are* our habits, and they are no longer deeply meaningful as specific ways to express and participate in the kingdom of God's unfolding in the world.

On the other hand, if we can maintain a clear understanding of how our practices are grounded in our core beliefs, that should allow us to appreciate rather than reject the ways other people have chosen to put those same beliefs into practice, even when their practices look somewhat different from ours.

This is a challenge facing every Christian group or denomination. It's not unique to Anabaptists. Every generation needs to have its own meaningful encounter with the living Christ and to respond to him by yielding its habits to his lordship.

NOTE: You can read more about the themes covered in this chapter in the following articles of the Confession of Faith in a Mennonite Perspective—*11: Baptism, 12: The Lord's Supper, 13: Foot washing, 14: Discipline in the church, 20: Truth and the avoidance of oaths, 21: Christian stewardship, 22: Peace, justice, and nonresistance.*

Chapter 9

Anabaptist Core Beliefs Today

Chapter 1 summarized the six core beliefs of Anabaptists as follows:
- **Jesus is Lord** over absolutely everything.
- The **kingdom of God** is where people unite under the lordship of Jesus.
- We **choose** to **follow** Jesus **together, surrendering our lives in love** like he did.

Chapters 2-8 reviewed the six core beliefs one at a time, noting their origins in the Scriptures and how they are explained in Anabaptist sources. I also reviewed many of the practices that have grown out of the core beliefs and suggested that they are all just different ways to make the core beliefs concrete and real in everyday life.

If, as Anabaptist Christians, we aspire to live New Testament Christian faith joyfully and faithfully in our daily lives, these beliefs should interweave with every part of our congregations' worship and teaching. They should be popping up everywhere and be hard to miss. If you are part of a Mennonite congregation, these core beliefs should sound very familiar to you, even if they are presented in slightly different language.

I urge Mennonite pastors and teachers to regularly review the links between our core beliefs and our practices. Let's make sure it's clear how our practices are grounded in our core beliefs, so that the answer to "Why do we do it this way?" is widely shared and broadly understood. This is especially important for children to learn, for new members to understand, and for everyone to remember. It's important to remember that our practices are more than just our habits. They are how we bring our core beliefs to life and how we play our part in living out the kingdom of God together in our local communities.

It might also be invigorating to occasionally review our practices to see if they are still the best way to express our core beliefs here and now. For example, in one congregation, while we continued to offer the usual opportunity for men to wash feet with men and women with women, we added a room where husbands and wives or families could wash feet together. We also added a hand washing station for people who could no longer kneel or whose feet were injured or damaged.

Some folks also began to ask if we could consider adding a practice that would be a closer parallel to what foot washing was in Jesus' day. They pointed out that, even though it made the disciples very uncomfortable to have Jesus wash their feet, the practice itself was not foreign to them. We began to wonder if there is a current practice that is more familiar to us than foot washing but which would typically only be done by a person of lower status. We're still working on that one.

Impact on the Broader Church

Over the 500 years since 1525, some of these practices have become broadly familiar to Christians across a wide range of denominations. For example, many evangelical Christians today are very familiar with the notion that *Christians have a responsibility to meet each other's needs*. This teaching predates the Anabaptists by many centuries, but they revived it with their emphasis on Christian community (following Jesus *together*). Many denominations and congregations now appoint "deacons" to coordinate this type of care for each other even if they don't strongly emphasize the broader teaching on Christian community as the visible expression of the kingdom of God in the world.

Most Christians today are also very familiar, at least in principle, with the importance of *witnessing to the truth of the gospel "in word and in deed."* Jesus forgave sins, but he also healed people's bodies. He said we need to be born again from within, but he also told an extended parable in Matthew 25 about the importance of meeting people's physical needs. Most Christian faith traditions continue to support both evangelistic mission work and relief and development work, seeking to offer a holistic presentation of good news.

At the same time, the Protestant reformers' emphasis on salvation as a primarily spiritual transaction for the individual created a tension that still lingers today. Evangelical Protestant Christians in particular tend to see "the gospel" as a message of forgiveness of individual sins that's primarily spread by preaching and church planting to produce more and more individual conversions. They also tend to see Christian efforts to provide relief or material aid, generate economic development, and seek justice as less important than evangelism.

From an Anabaptist perspective, this is all part of one announcement, since the reconciliation at the core of the gospel impacts all four broken relationships. As one author helpfully put it, individual regeneration is the *root* of the gospel; service and testimony to others is the *fruit* of the gospel (Smucker 1945, 14).

I will never forget a story I once heard Anabaptist theologian and author Ron Sider tell about his friend and brother in Christ, Pastor James Dennis of Philadelphia (Sider 1999, 24). Early in life, James Dennis was an angry black militant who was also abusing alcohol and ruining his marriage as he struggled to find stable work that allowed him to provide well for his family. He eventually ended up in prison after he committed a major crime. But during his time in prison, he came to personal faith in Jesus Christ. After his release, he joined a local congregation and was discipled by its pastor. Over time, as he cooperated with the Holy Spirit's work in his life, he got a good job, he bought a house, his marriage was restored, and he went on to become a pastor himself.

Sider asked, "Now does anybody really think that all Brother James needed was a better welfare system? Or a better job training program?" He answered, "Obviously that wasn't enough. He needed a living relationship with Jesus Christ at the core of his being. He needed to be transformed from the inside out. And the

Holy Spirit did that once he came to personal faith in Jesus Christ."

But Sider also asked, "Does anybody really think that Brother James's problems were all solved when he became a born-again Christian? What if he couldn't get a job or decent housing because he was black? What if the inner city schools only offered his children a lousy education? Obviously, he needed Jesus and a job. He needed evangelism and material social transformation." I never forgot that phrase—He needed Jesus and he needed a job. He needed good news in both word and deed.

Probably the most familiar and most widespread of all the Anabaptist core beliefs today is the emphasis on *faithful discipleship*—the simple idea that following Jesus should make a noticeable difference in someone's life. Most evangelical Christian groups now teach that the Holy Spirit works regeneration and transformation in the life of the believer if they cooperate with that work. They agree that our redemption isn't just something we claim and then add to our collection of personal treasures. It's the beginning of the power of God within us that enables us to follow Jesus in everyday life. I once heard historian Arnold Snyder say, "If Protestants have picked this up, they've become Anabaptists" (Snyder 2006). What a wonderful gift to have given to the broader Christian church.

Many discipling movements have emerged in recent decades. Examples include:
- An emphasis on life change in many megachurches, highlighted by brief testimonies. Rick Warren's *Purpose Driven Church* model presents "Christ-like character" as its central value and "changed lives" as its "source of legitimacy." (Warren 1995, 125) Warren's background is Southern Baptist.
- Dallas Willard's body of work has been focused on the importance of actually following Jesus in everyday life. His most elegant and profound presentation is in *Divine Conspiracy*. In his introduction, he writes, "This book . . . presents discipleship to Jesus as the very heart of the gospel." He says his goal is to challenge "the practical irrelevance of

actual obedience to Christ" for many Christians in the world today (Willard 1997, xvii, xv). Willard's background is Southern Baptist.
- The missional church movement has developed insightful teaching and specific tools designed to provide faith communities with a very clear answer to the question "What is your process for forming disciples?" This movement grew out of the Church of England.
- The central point of pastor Kyle Idelman's book *Not a Fan* is that Christians are called to be "completely committed" *followers* of Jesus, not just "enthusiastic admirers" of Jesus. Idelman's background is Church of Christ.

For me, one of the most intriguing movements that has emerged in the last several years is Missio Alliance. This organization gathers Christians from many denominations around "a common commitment to provide a place to address what faithfulness to Christ and His mission might look like for the churches of North America in the face of several new cultural challenges." If you browse through the "Focus," "Convictions," or "History" tabs on their website, it's striking how much the language they use reflects Anabaptist core beliefs: 1. Jesus is fully lord, 2. the kingdom of God, and 4. follow/discipleship. Their gatherings and resources have a distinctly Anabaptist tone, even though the organization's staff and leaders come from "across the Wesleyan, Baptist, Reformed, Holiness, Anglican, Charismatic, Anabaptist, and other traditions."

Many other Christian traditions have either adopted or been deeply impacted by Anabaptist beliefs and practices in the 500 years since they were first articulated. It's not unusual to find congregations today emphasizing one or more of the following:
- Deacons and/or benevolence funds to provide mutual aid
- Call to faithful discipleship
- Baptizing believers rather than infants
- Voluntary membership
- Small groups to build community

These beliefs and practices were unusual in the cultural context in which they were brought back to the attention of the church, but Anabaptists don't claim to be the only Christians who believe in or practice these things. We would just say that for us they are grounded in a specific framework of core beliefs which have then been expressed in these practices along with the other practices described throughout this book. For Anabaptists, it has always been about living out as faithfully as possible the teachings of Jesus and his apostles in the spirit in which they were intended.

Why Still Anti-Baptist!?

Several years ago, I realized I had stumbled onto a teaching moment when I heard a woman who has been a lifelong member of Mennonite churches refer to our congregation as "ANTI-baptist." In every class for new members after that, I wrote the two words on the board—ANTI-baptist and ANA-baptist—and made a point of crossing out the *anti* prefix on the first word as I explained the difference. I knew that if even a lifelong Mennonite was confusing these terms, she was not the only one doing so.

As I noted briefly in the introduction, the *ana* prefix comes from a Latin word that means to repeat or do again. The term *anabaptist* was originally intended as an insult by the critics and opponents of people who wanted to be "re"-baptized in the early 1500s, initially in Switzerland and southern Germany.

Of course, the "anabaptists" themselves considered their baptism as infants to be merely a custom of the church working closely with the local government rather than the baptism taught and practiced in the New Testament. For them, genuine Christian baptism had to follow a decision to turn from sin and to begin following Jesus, coupled with a conscious willingness to suffer if need be. To be faithful to the New Testament model and teaching, they wanted to be baptized as adult believers and called others to join them. So they became known as the Anabaptists (the re-baptizers), and the label has followed their heirs to the present day.

The various groups known today as "Baptist" trace their origin to England in the early 1600s, about 100 years later than the first Anabaptists, when very similar dynamics and convictions led a group of radical reformers to break away from the Church of England. Some historians suggest the early leaders were influenced by the Anabaptists, but the majority view among scholars is that this was not a very significant influence. They simply articulated very similar beliefs and practices in a different setting and formed a new movement when they began baptizing believers and established the first Baptist congregation in 1609.

Today there's an even wider range of emphases and practices among Baptists than among Anabaptists. Even though in general terms the two groups are fairly closely aligned on most points of doctrine, there are several meaningful differences that are often true. Here are a few:

In contrast to the Anabaptist core beliefs and practices presented here, Baptists generally . . .
- don't emphasize a kingdom of God perspective with reconciliation as the core of the good news Jesus came to proclaim
- place more emphasis on conversion (evangelism) than on discipleship (faithful following)
- place more emphasis on one's individual spiritual journey than on following Jesus together (Christian community)
- don't teach nonresistance or nonviolence

None of this means that Anabaptists are or ever were anti-Baptist! Baptists are among our closer cousins theologically, and we work closely with Baptists of many varieties in different mission and ministry settings. We just differ in our points of emphasis and the practices that flow from them.

Still out of Step

Probably the greatest continuing difference today between Anabaptists and evangelicals or Protestants is our commitment to the lordship of Jesus over the Scriptures as presented in chapter 2. We believe that the person, the work, and the lordship of Jesus are the essential key to all of what God has been doing, is doing, and will do in his creation.

Since the Bible tells the story of God's creation project, and since Jesus says so himself, we consider the life, teachings, example, death, resurrection, and lordship of Jesus to be the interpretive key to understanding the Bible. This "Christocentric" or Christ-centered way of reading and interpreting Scripture means that we aspire to align our beliefs and our practices as faithfully as possible with the example and teachings of Jesus. We reject interpretations of Scripture that lead us away from that aspiration, even when based on another part of the Bible.

This is not to set the Old (or "First") and New Testaments against each other. For Jesus, himself a Jew, the Hebrew Scriptures that we call the Old Testament *were* the Scriptures. Jesus thought and taught as a Jew formed by these Scriptures. At the same time, amid the many complexities of how to view and understand God and God's wishes for the world and for us, Anabaptists seek to be shaped in turn by Jesus' own understandings of his Scriptures and the way he taught them.

For example, Jesus says, "Love your enemies" (Matt. 5:44). We consider that more reliable guidance for our lives than the instructions God gave Joshua to destroy his enemies. When he says "Go and make disciples of all nations" (Matt. 28:19), and "Whoever does the will of my Father in heaven is my brother and sister and mother" (Matt. 12:50), we understand him to be rejecting earthly distinctions between us in the people of God, including national distinctions. This means we reject any teaching that calls us to destroy our enemies or that pits us against the people of other nations, since both of these contradict the teachings of Jesus.

Of the six core beliefs discussed here, the two that continue to create the most countercultural tension for Anabaptists in the United States and with many American Christians in the broader evangelical or Protestant churches are #5: We follow Jesus together (in loving community) and #6: We surrender our lives in love like Jesus did. These core beliefs generate the strongest critical responses from other Christians and are the main reasons why people, especially Americans, leave Anabaptist faith communities for other Christian groups. I addressed these tensions at length in the "It's not easy to live this way!" sections at the ends of chapters 6 and 7, but here are a few more thoughts:

As American culture continues to steep in individualism and as evangelical Christian teaching continues to focus primarily or only on helping individuals "get into heaven," the notion of following Jesus *together* seems increasingly strange or even nonsensical to Americans (Camp 2003, 103-104). Even our imagination for what that might look like begins to fade.

The irony is that, because human beings are made for relationship and connection, we all long for the richness of life provided by being embedded in a web of loving, trusting, intimate relationships. But if we adopt American cultural values and they are reinforced by the theology we are taught, we end up struggling to make the personal sacrifices required to sustain those types of relationships.

Even Anabaptists who remain in Anabaptist congregations, especially in the U.S., struggle with exactly this tension, too. To the extent that we adopt values and practices shaped by individualism, our experience of true Christian community within our congregations is weakened.

American culture also tends to prize individual success, triumph, and redemptive violence. We think individual achievement and distinction are essential to our sense of importance or significance as a person. Americans are winners! We are trained to think that the best way to deal with people or situations that interfere with our accomplishments is to destroy them. After all, they have intruded on our right to be all we can be.

The more deeply formed we are by these ideas, the more nonsensical it will sound to "surrender my life in love like Jesus did." For people who are repeatedly told in many different ways that redemptive violence in defending myself and my rights is the best solution to difficult situations, the notion that redemptive suffering is the truer, deeper solution and more faithful to the example and call of Jesus seems preposterous.

The idea that I would seek to become more humble, be eager to serve, or be willing to yield to another person or to a group seems completely bonkers to whole-hearted Americanism as generally expressed today. The resulting practices of nonresistance, rejection of violence, and foot washing seem completely out of step. The more fully we embrace the values of individual success and triumph and the practices that defend those values, the harder it will be for us to embrace the core belief of surrender and humility or to live it out in practice.

In the last decade or two, a third challenge has emerged in the U.S. that's creating increasing tension with core belief #2: the kingdom of God—the challenge of Christian nationalism. Even among Anabaptists, some who are troubled by real or perceived developments in the U.S. have been caught up in outrage or activism linked to a fear that the kingdom of God is losing ground in the public life and culture of the U.S.

In its presentation of the kingdom of God, chapter 3 provides a detailed rationale for why Christians (especially Anabaptists) reject or should reject Christian nationalism. I am convinced that the best defense against false ideas like these is to be so deeply formed by the teachings and example of Jesus and his apostles that we readily resist any other way of thinking or living that may attempt to seduce us.

Greg Boyd's book *The Myth of a Christian Nation* (Boyd 2005) provides an excellent and far more thorough treatment of the issues this raises than we have space for here. Let me just say that there's no basis in the New Testament for confusing the kingdom of God with any particular kingdom of the earth (with any particular nation-state). Whatever our interests or involvements may be as citizens of a particular nation state, our primary focus as followers of Jesus should be on faithfully living out the way of Jesus together in our daily lives and in our local settings, actively and noticeably loving our opponents (our enemies), and inviting anyone from any tribe or nation or people group to join us in that following. Any appeal or ideology or movement (like Christian nationalism) that draws us away from those activities is drawing us away from the way of Jesus.

Faithful to the End

I hope you now better understand the main point Harold Bender hoped to make in his *Anabaptist Vision* speech to academic historians when he said that even though contemporary notions of religious freedom (freedom of conscience), voluntarism in religion, and separation of church and state can be traced back to the Anabaptists, these don't define the essence of what they believed or the essence of who they were (Bender 1944, 4-5). Bender's argument was that those ideas and practices were grounded in underlying core beliefs drawn from the New Testament and that the core beliefs were meant to reflect the true intent of the teachings of Jesus and his apostles as faithfully as possible.

This book has been my attempt to make that same point for a general audience, which is that Anabaptist practices are grounded in our core beliefs. To truly understand or to honestly critique the practices, you need to start with understanding the core beliefs and how they give rise to the practices.

The more important issue for a critic is whether you agree or disagree that the core beliefs are faithful to the spirit, intent, and content of the teachings of Jesus and his apostles. If you reject one or more of the core beliefs, of course you will reject the practices derived from them. But if you embrace the core beliefs, your objections will have mostly to do with how the core beliefs are applied or expressed.

In that case, you may not subscribe to how a particular group is living out the core beliefs (e.g., you might not be prepared to join the Amish), but you will understand and respect the underlying rationale for their way of life, and you will be seeking to express the core beliefs in your own way.

Acknowledgments

As with most books, this one has been in gestation a long time—over fifteen years! I am grateful to see it completed. My perspective on Anabaptist life and thought has been formed by many situations and relationships over even more years than that. There are too many of them to name or thank here, but their influence has been profound and much appreciated.

Having said that, I am deeply grateful to everyone who has worked with me to help bring this book to press.

Thank you to the Fransen Family Foundation for your financial support as part of your ongoing work to encourage commitment to Jesus Christ and to Anabaptist teachings. I am honored to join you in that mission.

Thank you to the congregation of Mount Joy Mennonite Church and my colleagues there for helping me test an early version of these ideas.

Thank you especially to all the first readers who gave me such helpful feedback and whose comments greatly improved the final product—Shelley Baker, William Higgins, Gerry Keener, Jason Kuniholm, Nita Landis, Miriam Locklair, Kevin Milligan, Sarah Milligan, Brinton Rutherford, and Reid Telando. Brinton and William were especially helpful on the theological framing, and Sarah's careful eye was a huge help in cleaning up my grammar.

A special thank you to Nita, who patiently reread and commented again and again on various sections of the book and whose encouragement has been invaluable along the way.

Thank you, too, to Michael A. King of Cascadia Publishing House LLC. Your knowledge, expertise, and editorial guidance kept me on track, and your patient encouragement during the long gestation process was incredibly helpful and much appreciated.

References and Resources for Further Study

These resources will be helpful to you if you want to do further study. The first group includes sources mentioned or quoted in earlier chapters. The second group includes other fine summaries of Anabaptist core beliefs. You can find summaries and responses and discussions of these resources online.

Resources Referenced in This Book

Bender, Harold S., 1944. *The Anabaptist Vision.* Herald Press.
> A very important and influential framing of the Anabaptist perspective. Printed as a 35-page booklet summarizing core beliefs 4, 5, and 6. See below for more detail.

Benner, David, 2003. *Surrender to Love: Discovering the Heart of Christian Spirituality.* IVP Books.
> A brief exploration of the themes of love and surrender at the heart of Christian spirituality. God invites us to respond to his perfect love with complete surrender and trust.

Bonhoeffer, Dietrich, 1963. *The Cost of Discipleship,* 2nd ed. Macmillan.

Boyd, Gregory A., 2005. *The Myth of a Christian Nation: How the Quest for Political Power Is Destroying the Church.* Zondervan.
> Excellent, concise distinction between "the kingdom of the cross" framed by redemptive suffering and "the kingdom of the sword" framed by redemptive violence. As a pastor, Boyd wrestles with daily implications of navigating dual citizenship in these kingdoms.

Braght, Thieleman J. van, 1951. *Martyrs Mirror*, 5th ed. Mennonite Publishing House. First published in 1660.

Camp, Lee, 2003. *Mere Discipleship: Radical Christianity in a Rebellious World*. Brazos Press. An excellent and helpful presentation of the basics of the Christian message from an Anabaptist perspective.

Confession of Faith in a Mennonite Perspective, 1995. Herald Press.

An updated statement of Anabaptist theology (from a Mennonite perspective) in 24 articles. Available online or in booklet form.

Freeman, Curtis, James McClendon, Rosalee Velloso Ewell, 1999. "Balthasar Hubmaier: On Infant Baptism Against Oecolampad," 32-40 and "Takashi Yamada," 362-368, in *Baptist Roots: A Reader in the Theology of a Christian People*. Judson Press.

Hershberger, Michele, 2013. *God's Story, Our Story: Exploring Christian Faith and Life*, rev. ed. Herald Press. See below for more detail.

Jenkins, Philip, 2014. *The Great and Holy War: How World War 1 Became a Religious Crusade*. Harper One.

Kraybill, Donald B., 2003. *The Upside Down Kingdom*, 3rd ed. Herald Press.

A careful review of eleven ways the kingdom of God looks upside down from within the kingdom of the world.

Lewis, C. S., 1952. *Mere Christianity*. Macmillan Publishing Company.

McKnight, Scot, 2007. *A Community Called Atonement: Living Theology*. Abingdon Press.

Excellent and eloquent presentation of the four broken relationships and the formation of a reconciled community as the focus of the atonement, which is the basis for the title. McKnight argues that many explanations of the atonement are far too narrow and fail to capture the full breadth of meaning for the atonement that's presented in the New Testament.

Neufeld, Vernon, 1983. *If We Can Love: The Mennonite Mental Health Story*. Faith and Life Press. Quoted by Aaron Levin in "Mennonite Mental Health System: Practicing What They Preach." *Psychiatric News*, 19 May 2006. https://doi.org/10.1176/pn.41.10.0018

Philips, Dirk, 1557. "The Incarnation of Jesus Christ." Reprinted in Walter Klaassen and A. B. Kolb, 1966. *Enchiridion*, 97-100. Quoted in Walter Klaassen, ed., 1981. *Anabaptism in Outline*, 36. Herald Press.

Riedeman, Peter, 1542. *Account of Our Religion, Doctrine, and Faith*, 22-26. Reprinted (1950) Hodder and Stoughton. Quoted in Walter Klaassen, ed. *Anabaptism in Outline*, 31.

Ruth, John L., 2001. *The Earth Is the Lord's: A Narrative History of the Lancaster Mennonite Conference*. Herald Press.

———. 2021. *This Very Ground, This Crooked Affair: A Mennonite Homestead on Lenape Land*. Cascadia Publishing House.

Schaeufele, Wolfgang, 1962. "The Missionary Vision and Activity of the Anabaptist Laity," *Mennonite Quarterly Review* 36: 99-115.

Sider, Ronald J., 1999. *Good News and Good Works: A Theology for the Whole Gospel*. Baker Books.

Simons, Menno, 1534. *Brief Confession on the Incarnation*. 1534. Reprinted in *The Complete Writings of Menno Simons*, 419-454. Herald Press. 1984.

———. *Foundation of Christian Doctrine*. 1539. Reprinted in *The Complete Writings of Menno Simons*, 103-226.

———. *Confession of the Triune God*. 1550. Reprinted in *The Complete Writings of Menno Simons*, 487-498. Paraphrased Smucker. 1945: 9.

———. *Reply to Gellius Faber*. 1554. Reprinted in *The Complete Writings of Menno Simons*, 623-781. Paraphrased Smucker, 1945: 10.

Smith, Christian, 2012. *The Bible Made Impossible: Why Biblicism Is Not a Truly Evangelical Reading of Scripture*. Brazos Press.

Smith, James K. A., 2016. *You are What You Love: The Spiritual Power of Habit*. Brazos Press.

Smucker, Donovan, 1945. "The Theological Triumph of the Early Anabaptist Mennonites: The Rediscovery of Biblical Theology in Paradox," *Mennonite Quarterly Review* 19(1): 5-26.

Snyder, C. Arnold, 1995. *Anabaptist History and Theology: An Introduction*. Pandora Press / Herald Press.

———, 1999. *From Anabaptist Seed: The Historical Core of Anabaptist-Related Identity*. Pandora Press / Herald Press. A 50-page booklet on "a common core of conviction and practice in early Anabaptism" for Mennonite World Conference

———, 2004. *Following in the Footsteps of Christ: The Anabaptist Tradition*. Orbis Books.

———, 2006. "The Anabaptist Path." Oral presentation to Lancaster Mennonite Conference (LMC) leaders in a leadership development seminar. April 27, 2006. Lancaster, Pennsylvania.

Stafford, Tim, 2005. "The Church—Why Bother? There Is No Healthy Relationship with Jesus Without a Relationship to the Church." *Christianity Today*, January, 49 (1): 42-49

Swartley, Willard M., 2013. *Believers Church Bible Commentary: John*. Herald Press.

Warren, Rick, 1995. *The Purpose Driven Church: Growth Without Compromising Your Message and Mission*. Zondervan.

———, 2002. *The Purpose Driven Life: What on Earth Am I Here For?* Zondervan.

Wilder, Jim, 2020. *Renovated: God, Dallas Willard, and the Church that Transforms.* NavPress/ Tyndale House Publishers

Willard, Dallas, 1997. *The Divine Conspiracy: Rediscovering our Hidden Life in God.* HarperSanFrancisco.

A profound reflection on the meaning and importance of Christian discipleship and the methods that produce mature followers of Jesus. Not a short or easy read (at 400 pages!), but a masterpiece.

Wright, N. T., 2016, originally 2012. *How God Became King: The Forgotten Story of the Gospels.* HarperOne. A compelling kingdom perspective on the purposes of God.

Zerbe, Gordon, 2016. *Believers Church Bible Commentary: Philippians.* Herald Press.

Resources for Further Study: Other Summaries of Anabaptist Core Beliefs

Bender, Harold, 1944. *The Anabaptist Vision.* Herald Press.

Harold Bender wrote this brief summary in three days. It was his presidential address to the American Society of Church History in December 1943. Bender hoped to convince his academic colleagues to take Anabaptists seriously as true reformers rather than dismissing them as extremists focused mainly on gaining freedom of religion and the separation of church and state. Bender agreed that the Anabaptists called for those things, but said those issues don't define the essence of what they believed or the essence of who they were.

The Anabaptist Vision was not written to be a thorough or systematic presentation of all of Anabaptist belief and practice. Bender only realized after the fact that he had provided fellow Mennonites with a new and more positive self-definition. His *Anabaptist Vision* was a dynamic and theologically rich alternative to Mennonite statements that were more focused on doctrine and discipline.

I highlighted Bender's three elements of the Anabaptist Vision in earlier chapters, including them as core beliefs 4, 5, and 6:

Discipleship as the essence of Christian faith
  (chapter 5: #4 Follow)

Brotherhood [today *Peoplehood*] of love in the church
  (chapter 6: #5 Together/ Community)

Love and nonresistance / peace in all relationships
  (chapter 7: #6 Surrender)

I am convinced that Bender assumed the importance of core beliefs 1: the lordship of Jesus and 2: the kingdom of God, even though he didn't explicitly discuss them—you can only include so much in a presidential address after all. He did say the lordship of Christ is the basis for committing oneself to whole life discipleship (p. 20). He also briefly mentioned core belief 3: Choose in the section on the Anabaptist's "new concept of the church" when he talked about "voluntary church membership" based on true conversion and including a commitment to discipleship (p.24).

Dintaman, Stephen, 1992. "The Spiritual Poverty of the Anabaptist Vision." *The Conrad Grebel Review.* Spring, 10:205-208.

In this widely discussed and frequently reprinted article, Dintaman noted that in the way it is stated, Bender's Anabaptist vision is essentially behavioral. Dintaman discerned two unstated assumptions behind Bender's vision, 1.) basic evangelical doctrines about the being and work of God in Christ, and 2.) that living out this vision was only possible through the indwelling presence of Christ and the power of the Holy Spirit. Because the teachers who came after Bender failed to keep these assumptions at the forefront, Dintaman believed, Mennonite practice drifted into a focus on proper behavior rather than on the reasons and sources for that behavior.

Dintaman lamented that Bender's statement didn't include a statement of the gospel or a clear grounding of the vision's behaviors in the regenerating power and work of the Holy Spirit. He was also concerned that over time this approach can lead us to think that our redemption is something we accomplish for God rather than something he accomplishes for us.

Camp, Lee, 2003. *Mere Discipleship.* Brazos Press.

An Anabaptist presentation of "the basic Christian message" inspired by and in some ways responding to C. S. Lewis's *Mere Christianity*. Camp, a student of John Howard Yoder, very helpfully translates Yoder's perspectives for a more general audience. This is an excellent resource, even if the reading level and length make it a bit more challenging than Lewis's book.

Roth, John, 2005; *Beliefs.* 2007; *Stories.* 2009. *Practices.* Herald Press.

Each of these roughly 200 page books is well written and well worth studying. In *Beliefs*, Roth focuses on four distinctive beliefs of Mennonites: 1.) reading scripture through the example and teachings of Jesus, 2.) believers baptism, 3.) faith as discipleship, and 4.) the visible church. As you know by now, my perspective is that all of these flow from even deeper core beliefs.

Stories recounts the historical origins of the Mennonite faith tradition (Roth is a historian) and follows immigration routes throughout Europe, to south Russia, to North America, and then around the world, setting most of the components of our faith tradition in their historical contexts. *Practices* reviews Mennonite worship and witness, that is, how we bear witness to the love and power of God in all the various aspects of our lives. Roth offers a very detailed and nuanced discussion of how we put our beliefs into practice in everyday life.

Hershberger, Michele, 2013. *God's Story, Our Story*, rev. ed. Herald Press.

A very helpful presentation of the beliefs and practices explained in the *Confession of Faith*, setting them in the context and flow of the historical narrative of the biblical story. I used this as a primary resource for the preparation classes I led for baptism and new members. It's well written and very readable, but at 170 pages it was more content than most participants were used to reading. Better suited for a 6-8 week class than a 6-8 hour seminar.

Neufeld, Alfred, 2015. *What We Believe Together*, 2nd ed. Good Books.

This book expands on the 2006 statement adopted by Mennonite World Conference which summarizes the shared convictions of Anabaptist related churches around the world. The introduction and wording of the seven convictions mixes beliefs and practices together in ways I find confusing. The statement packs a tremendous amount of content into its few brief lines. Beliefs and practices are also discussed in intermingled ways in the chapters of the book.

The introduction mentions reconciliation in Jesus Christ by the grace of God followed by statements about 1.) God as trinity; 2.) Jesus; 3.) church as community, the lordship of Jesus, believer baptism, and discipleship; 4.) the Bible; 5.) the empowering (Holy) Spirit of Jesus, peacemaking, nonviolence, justice, mutual aid; 6.) worship, Lords' Supper, preaching, mutual accountability; and 7.) worldwide community of faith that crosses all earthly boundaries, creation care, inviting everyone to know Jesus Christ as savior and lord. The conclusion mentions Jesus's second coming and the final fulfillment of God's kingdom.

Murray, Stuart, 2010. *The Naked Anabaptist*. Herald Press.

Murray identifies seven core "convictions" of Anabaptists that "spell out what it means for many Anabaptists today to identify with this tradition." Murray wrote the book to provide guidance and clarity for the Anabaptist Network in the United Kingdom, so his focus is more on what it means to be Anabaptist in the U.K. than on providing a structured presentation of the whole framework. He is writing mostly for believers who are newly emerging from the blend of church and state that continues to deeply shape Christian experience and imagination in the U.K.

Here are Murray's seven core convictions, which he offers as something of a rallying point or manifesto for the Anabaptist Network in the U.K.

1. Jesus is Lord and center of our faith. We are committed to worshipping him and following him.

2. Jesus is the focal point of God's revelation, so we are committed to a Jesus-centered approach to the Bible.

3. Western culture is emerging from Christendom, that is, we are rediscovering the separation of church and state.

4. We are committed to be good news to the poor, powerless, and persecuted, turning away from our attachment to status, wealth, and force.

5. Churches should be committed communities of worship, discipleship, and mission.

6. We are called to live simply, share generously, care for creation, and work for justice.

7. Peace is at the heart of the gospel. We are committed to nonviolence and to finding nonviolent alternatives in resolving conflicts.

Becker, Palmer, 2017. *Anabaptist Essentials*. Herald Press.

Becker's focus over many years of serving as a missionary, pastor, and teacher has been much the same as mine in this book—providing a concise and memorable summary of Anabaptist essentials for a general audience. He approaches this body of thought from a different angle than I do, but makes many of the same observations. This is a rich resource and highly recommended.

Here is Becker's basic framework, summarized in three pithy statements, which he calls "core values":

1. Jesus is the center of our faith—His lordship means we read scripture through his example and teachings, and we follow him (discipleship).

2. Community is the center of our life—We forgive each other (because God has forgiven us), discern God's will together, and hold each other accountable (discipline).

3. Reconciliation is the center of our work—We are reconciled with God (and transformed by the power of the Holy Spirit), with each other in Christian community, and seek to resolve conflict nonviolently.

One of Becker's final chapters stresses the Holy Spirit's presence and work in animating this approach to Christian life and thought. Becker agrees with Dinataman that the power of God at work within us transforms us and enables us to be Jesus' faithful followers.

The Author

Karl R. Landis serves as a pastor, author, teacher, and coach, mostly in Mennonite and other Anabaptist contexts. His greatest joy comes from translating complex ideas or insights into more accessible content for learners of all sorts. As an avid reader and learner himself, he is able to draw on a wide range of experience and wisdom.

Landis currently serves as an interim pastor and as a chair with Convene, coaching a group of Christian business leaders. He was previously lead pastor of Mount Joy Mennonite Church after serving as Director of Leadership Development for Lancaster Mennonite Conference (now LMC). In these roles over more than twenty years, he has taught and written on leadership, theology, Bible, church history, and Christian living for adult learners, ESL learners, undergraduates, and graduate students.

Landis holds a Master of Theological Studies degree from Gordon-Conwell Theological Seminary and a PhD and MA in Sociology from the University of Michigan. He completed his undergraduate study at Messiah College and Temple University.

Landis started his cross-cultural and interdenominational journey at age five in Central America as the son of Mennonite missionaries. Since then, he has lived in four countries and five U.S. states and enjoyed worship and friendship with Christians ranging from Quakers to Roman Catholics to Eastern Orthodox.

www.ingramcontent.com/pod-product-compliance
Lightning Source LLC
Chambersburg PA
CBHW020332170426
43200CB00006B/353